Peoplework

Peoplework

Communications Dynamics for Librarians

Judith W. Powell
and
Robert B. LeLieuvre

American Library Association
Chicago 1979

Library of Congress Cataloging in Publication Data

Powell, Judith W
    Peoplework, communications dynamics
    for librarians.

    Includes bibliographies and index.
    1. Libraries and readers. 2. Interpersonal
communication. 3. Librarians—Psychology.
I. LeLieuvre, Robert B., joint author. II. Title.
Z711.P68   020   79-18018
ISBN 0-8389-0290-1

Printed in the United States of America

Cover design by Howard Solotroff

This book is dedicated to
Constance K. Finnegan,
whose love for people
showed clearly in every part
of her library work.

I see communication as a huge
umbrella that covers and affects all
that goes on between human beings.
Once a human being has arrived on
this earth, *communication is the
largest single factor determining
what kinds of relationships he makes
with others and what happens to him
in the world about him.* How he
manages his survival, how he
develops intimacy, how productive
he is, how he makes sense, how he
connects with his own divinity—all
are largely dependent on his
communication skills . . . . *All*
communication is learned . . . .
Once a person realizes that all of
his communication is learned, he
can set about changing it if he
wants to.

—Virginia Satir, *Peoplemaking*
(Palo Alto, Calif.: Science and
Behavior Books, 1972), pp. 30–31.

Contents

v

Figures

Introduction

The outcome of any number of important, even crucial, human interactions depends upon successful communication. Too often chance plays a larger role than conscious choice in the outcome of such interactions. We have written this book with the firm belief that such a course of events is not inevitable.

We began this venture after having discovered that we share some basic assumptions. The first is that most people not only *need* to communicate but also wish to do so effectively. That is, they want to give and to receive messages that are appropriate and helpful within the context of both their personal and working lives. We also share, however, the belief that many, if not most, people are neither generally nor formally taught the very important concepts and skills they need to know to communicate. What they do learn is often incidentally incorporated, but not necessarily understood, as a result of observing the varying, sometimes contradictory and confusing, models their parents, teachers, and peers provide along the way.

This book is directed to librarians because communication of all kinds is the reason libraries and media centers exist. We do not feel that it is assuming too much to say that librarians, media specialists, and others should be the first to see the importance of knowledge and skills in interpersonal and group communication as a natural extension of their own work. There are two other positive factors that make librarians particularly suited to becoming involved in what we have to offer. First, communication work involves evaluative criteria. Our book provides criteria for evaluating models of communication similar in many ways to the criteria used by librarians reviewing and selecting media. Second, we ask our readers to adopt an eclectic view of communication. Librarians always have known that there are many sides to a question and have sought to provide such for the public. Here we ask them to engage in open-minded self-education, which public and school libraries have offered the general public since their beginning.

One author of this book is a librarian, and the other is a psychologist. These two professions are interrelated, both concerned with life-long learning. Psychologists are frequently involved in education; many consider themselves educators because they see total life experience as a learning process, and view communication as the single most essential vehicle for learning. Librarians are frequently considered educators, particularly in the Rogerian sense of acting as "facilitators" in the learning process. Therefore, the word "facilitator" will be used in this sense in the book. The others in the education world, particularly teachers working in many United States schools, are now learning about and using new, humanistic approaches to communication. Librarians should certainly not ignore the potential provided by these skills in the practice of their profession, any more than they should ignore the metric system or the impending energy crisis. Various names have been applied to these new approaches to learning (i.e., humanistic education, affective education, confluent education, etc.). Regardless of the name used, five major goals are crucial at all levels of education. These are: (1) to increase self-awareness; (2) to develop feelings of self-worth; (3) to refine the abilities of thinking and of problem solving; (4) to enhance creativity; and (5) to explore and choose values. Thus, successful learning at all levels involves growth in all of these areas.

In the past ten years, many writers have placed before an eager public the necessary tools to successfully plumb the carefully guarded secrets of trades and professions. There has been a renaissance of the pioneer philosophy of sharing, of making available to neighbors, relatives, and friends information that makes life work better. Such books have achieved success because they simplify highly technical language, thereby making both the vocabulary and the information available to all. Professions such as law and medicine have been demythologized in this way. *The People's Pharmacy* (New York: St. Martin's Press, 1976) is an example of such a book.

This book is called PEOPLEWORK. It is an attempt to demythologize the psychology and communication requirements and dynamics that are important both in human relationships and in library service. Libraries are successful because of the people who staff them and their relationships to other people. To be more specific, librarians form the human connection between people and the information or knowledge they need. Acting as that necessary link, librarians are learning designs and references.

Finally, believing in equal rights for women, the authors are concerned with the "he-she" pronoun problem, and so have decided to alternate the use of "he" and "she" by chapter. In many cases this has worked out quite naturally, with "she" used by the female coauthor, "he" by the male. In areas written in collaboration, the problem has been worked out as fairly and naturally as possible. For those who feel uncomfortable about "she" as a singular pronoun in the generic case, the authors recommend the book *Women and Words*, by Casey Miller and Kate Swift (New York: Doubleday-Anchor Books, 1977) for a better understanding of the need for this change.

Our acknowledgments: to Carlista Berry, who persevered at the typewriter and helped complete the manuscript on schedule; to the Waterville School System, whose board of education and administrators gave a gift of time to this project; to the members of the library media center staff of Waterville High School—Anita, Connie, Jackie, Jim, Marguerite, Merle, and Thelma—who have contributed to this book in so many ways; to Chris Taylor, who made an excellent substitute; to Ruth Bailey at the Maine State Library, for small favors; to Cam Flower, Martha Mitchell, and Glenys Gifford for their research assistance at the University of Maine's Fogler and Mantor Libraries; to Goddard College for encouraging us to embark on the first project that led eventually to this one.

And finally, our special affection and thanks are due Laima, Richard, Sandy, Gregory, Wendy, and Sabrina, who each in his or her own way saw us through and who understand what this book means to us. We are grateful for their patience!

1 A Neglected Basic Skill

Answering the "Whats" and the "So-Whats" about Affective Education

The Scene: Room 209, the State Office Building. A hearing is in progress before the Senate Legal Affairs Committee. At issue is Bill 894, sponsored by a freshman senator. The room is full, hot, and stuffy as are so many legislative hearing rooms; it is charged with emotion because the bill in question proposes legal action against anyone knowingly distributing obscene materials to minors. All the old questions are being asked and argued here. What is obscene? Who will make a judgment to determine which material is obscene? What can be done about the proliferation of "smut" and its increasing availability to the young? Can children and young adults be hurt by reading materials that are obscene? What about censorship? What about the basic freedoms Americans are guaranteed by the Constitution?

The battle lines are clearly drawn at this point. Rational arguments offered by both sides play only a small role in what is happening. On one side of the aisle the bill's proponents are sitting, waiting their turn to speak, their opportunity to support those now testifying. The members of this group are concerned parents, officers of women's clubs, and representatives of churches and religious organizations. On the other side sit civil libertarians, bookstore owners, book distributors, teachers, and librarians, as well as representatives from state bodies that govern public education and libraries. The two groups are galvanized and, while there is no real fear of physical violence, there is

1

visible animosity and anger present in the room. It is as if two teams were in the midst of a very important, very close game in which there have already been some bad plays, some close calls, some unnecessary roughness, and some unfair refereeing.

The hearing lasts all afternoon and could easily extend into the evening hours. The legislature, however, is reconvening; people who have not yet been heard are requested to submit their testimony in writing if they wish to do so. A great many people leave the meeting feeling frustrated and threatened. Nothing is resolved.

Anyone who works in a library and anyone involved in education knows how sticky the whole issue of obscenity can be. Perhaps, however, they have not yet connected it with the subject of this chapter, affective education. Controversies over what should or should not be taught to children usually involve the value system of the society in which the children live. Emotions run high when values are challenged. Affective education deals with values. Furthermore, it is concerned with the areas of feelings, communication skills, and group dynamics. Obviously this senate hearing is a prime example of a group at work, of a communication process, of feelings, and of a clash of values. The following pages will point out that an understanding of communication skills and functional group work by the participants might well have changed the whole tone and tenor of the hearing.

Consider the possibility that one of the most important basic processes, one of the most important survival skills in today's society, has been neglected in education. Another "basic," in addition to the standard reading, writing, and computational skills, has been left out of the curriculum in most schools; the mastering of this neglected basic skill might well solve many of the problems of today's world. This basic area is affective communication—the subject of this book.

The authors find it amazing, indeed incredible, that knowledge of the affective domain has been left to chance when so much is at stake. Over and over again in serious editorials, learned articles, and comic television portrayals, as well as in tragic news stories, the family and its problems as a social unit in society are noted. This nation's communication with nations of different cultural backgrounds has become increasingly complex; differing groups within the country have interacted with increasing anger. From strikes to walkouts, from Watergate to the syndicate, from juvenile drug problems to sociopathic or psychotic terrorists, it is obvious that something is dreadfully amiss. This book will demonstrate how certain kinds of listening and speaking and certain expressions of feelings play an important role in learning and problem solving. It will show the common thread, the logic, and the pragmatic approaches used by many of the models of human communication. Finally, it will illustrate how these theories and practices can be incorporated into everyone's life style in ways that will not ask for radical changes in basic beliefs or philosophies.

Humanistic Education

At this time, a rather informal time line will be presented, along with some background information on the areas of affective communication that form the view of humanistic education that will be discussed in succeeding chapters. The groupings are somewhat arbitrary; the judgments and critical analyses are the authors'. Some models are doubtlessly missing, and some aspects of the models included may not be emphasized as much as others. Time and space will not allow coverage of all events or of all people in this rapidly growing area. So, with all due respect to John Dewey and others who may have been missed, here is a list of the groupings, theories, practical approaches, and people of affective humanistic education: (1) Jones, Brown, Samples, and the Confluent model; (2) Krathwohl, Bloom, Raths, Masia, Simon, and the Values Clarification model; (3) Perls, Rogers, Maslow, and the Self-Awareness/Self-Esteem models; (4) Berne, Glasser, Gordon, and the Problem-Solving Skills models; and (5) Cartwright, Zander, Schmuck, Schmuck, and the Group Dynamics model.

The definition of "affective" used here involves the ways that human beings deal with their feelings, attitudes, and values. Such a definition indicates that human beings have been involved in affective education to some degree far back in history. Whenever it was that people first "got religion," whenever it was that they first began trying to determine what was "good or bad," whenever value judgments were first made, enforced, suggested, or taught—there began the first affective involvement in either self-education or education of others.

In the United States, however, because of the issue of separation of church and state, the systematic teaching of values and moral philosophies in public schools has sometimes been evaded. In doing so, the areas of feelings and attitudes have been shunned as well, since they seemed at times to be closely connected with values taught in churches. Today there is a growing concern among some religious groups and among parents that, indeed, morals ought to be taught in the schools. This debate, closely connected to those on obscenity and censorship, is still very unsettled.

At the present time, a person's religious beliefs are politely respected in most public schools, and discussion or debate of those beliefs is carefully avoided. This situation occurs not only because of the separation of church and state, but also because most individuals do not think of religious issues as open to testing or to grading. A person's religion and its concomitant value structure are not considered subjects for outside inspection or evaluation. The question frequently asked is: If schools become involved in the affective domain, are they not encroaching on religious territory? If there is a real boundary between religious and affective education, that line is too fine for some people, and for others it simply does not exist.

Just as there are individuals who have trouble with the religious implications of affective education, there are those who have difficulty with the psychological ones. Some teachers and parents, for instance, are concerned that affective education involves a kind of tampering— not with the soul, but with the psyche. These people have visions of therapy done without consent, mind control, behavior control, and experimentation. Perhaps they worry about classroom-induced neuroses or psychotic episodes triggered by amateur teacher-therapists. For these reasons and others, affective humanistic education has been considered "too hot to handle" in many schools.

The background necessary for understanding affective humanistic education begins with the scholarly work of Bloom, Engelhart, Furst, Hill, and Krathwohl (1956), and of Krathwohl, Bloom, and Masia (1964). These authors were concerned with building separate taxonomies of educational objectives for the cognitive and the affective domains. They realized that the objectives would not necessarily be the same. This concept was, in a sense, revolutionary, since education even to this day in some quarters consists of the belief that "if cognitive objectives are developed, there will be a corresponding development of appropriate affective behaviors" (Krathwohl et al., 1964, p. 20). Perhaps this was a way of rationalizing away the need to help children in school deal with their emotions. The authors were not as concerned with the feelings and the attitudes of children as they were with the importance of identifying and working with values in the educational process. The interesting fact about their taxonomies, however, is that although their work began in the 1940s and although the first handbook on the cognitive domain was published in 1956, the second handbook on the affective domain did not appear for eight more years, in 1964. The authors offer as reasons the "lack of clarity in the statement of affective objectives that we have found in the literature" (Krathwohl et al., p. 13), as well as their own concern that there were few "examiners" on the college level who could see any use for a taxonomy of the affective domain. Apparently they were hesitant to push work concerning affective education upon a still reluctant audience. Yet in the second handbook the authors discussed their recognition as far back as 1948 of the need for achievement testing of educational objectives, "defined in terms of thoughts, feelings, and actions," that included a wide range of human responses such as "having an attitude towards some object or process" (Krathwohl et al., pp. 3–4). They credit the research of Jacob (1957), however, in giving them the needed impetus to finish the work of the second part of the taxonomy. From Jacob they concluded, "The evidence suggests that affective behaviors develop when appropriate learning experiences are provided for students much the same as cognitive behavior is developed from appropriate learning experiences" (Krathwohl et al., p. 20).

The Confluent Education Model

In the late 1950s and early 1960s a great many changes were initiated in American education. College professors, psychologists, scientists, and teachers began devising new teaching approaches, particularly but not entirely in the area of the sciences. Although most people were uncomfortable with the truth of the matter, this sudden shift in emphasis to science was obviously a reaction to Russia's apparent scientific superiority in space during the Sputnik scare.

It would seem, with this new focus on the basic sciences, that affective education would surely be sidetracked in the race for the moon and, in a way, it was. Jerome Bruner, one of the leading educational psychologists and then a professor at Harvard, seemed to understand the need for looking at more than just the teaching of science. He said at the Woods Hole conference, the first gathering of American scientists and educators after Sputnik, "It has been our conviction in planning the conference that it would be unwise to limit ourselves exclusively to the teaching of science, that the eventual problem would be more general than that, and that it would be in the interest of perspective to compare the issues involved in teaching science with those in a more humanistic field such as history" (Bruner, 1960, p. x). Bruner, however, was talking about the content of history as humanistic; he was not optimistic that affective processes could be incorporated with cognitive content.

Affective education finally was linked to the new curriculum being developed by educators, psychologists, and teachers through the work of Richard M. Jones. At the Endicott Conference, held at the Massachusetts Institute of Technology in 1962, the designing of an innovative social studies curriculum and the incorporating of a new theory of instruction, as inspired by Bruner, was initiated. Jones, a longtime champion of affective education, became the gadfly of this conference, attempting to bring attention to his concerns that educators heed the need for understanding a child's emotions and feelings. He was dismissed by scientists who misunderstood his words and were fearful of psychiatric intrusion into education. Jones described his encounter with a well-known educator attending that conference in the following way:

> ... one of the nation's most prestigious scientist-educators rose
> to urge the assembly to disregard my remarks, as they represented
> for him the narrowness of vision he had learned to expect "from
> psychiatrists." "Unless they can render their data into indices
> of pathology and sickness," he said, "they are helpless before it."
> He urged the membership, therefore, "To be man enough" not
> to be diverted from its task by these "psycho-phantisms." So, I
> thought, it has come to this. The clinician says "emotions" and
> "fantasy" and the educator hears "pathology and sickness."
> [Jones, pp. 9–10]

Briefly, Jones's theory of affective education maintained that a person's feelings, values, and attitudes are always part of his thought processes, consciously or unconsciously. In fact, the intellect, emotions, and fantasies are inextricably interwoven. Jones urged, as did George Isaac Brown (1971) and Bob Samples (1976), that educators recognize the need for an integrated curriculum, one that permits the full and creative development of human beings. The work of Ornstein (1972) and Samples relates to a fuller understanding of consciousness, creative ability, and the functions of the brain—particularly the right hemisphere. Ornstein was convinced that Western cognition, Western thought has blocked out and limited some of the individual's ways of knowing about self and the world. He stressed the importance of meditation and yoga techniques for developing a complete self-awareness and cosmic consciousness. Samples argued the importance of intuition, emotion, and creative consciousness to education. His work with right hemisphere–learning indicates the cyclical patterns of alternation between play and tasks that children need and so create when they move step-by-step through a problem-solving sequence. Such a position supports Jones's notion of confluent education.

In the 1960s and early 1970s something else was also happening to education. A small but articulate group of educators were so upset by what they saw happening in schools that they were in favor of abolishing schools altogether (e.g., Illich, 1971). Others wanted to restructure the system. Men such as James Herndon (1972), John Holt (1964, 1967, 1972), and Jonathan Kozol (1967, 1975) wrote powerful and touching books on what they witnessed and experienced as teachers.

They described the unproductive environment of the particular schools in which they worked and, in some cases, the distressing and unhappy environment in which their students lived. They recognized all too well the importance of helping children take their place in a competitive society. They were aware of the need for students to master the basic skills and competencies of reading, writing, and computation. They also wanted them to learn how to think for themselves, to learn how to learn, to understand their feelings, and to go on thinking, learning, and feeling for the rest of their lives. They did not believe children could learn well if they were not treated as whole human beings whose feelings, attitudes, and values were taken into account. They were angry or disillusioned because they had found too often that, in spite of their own personal commitment to students, the school system in which they worked had not been responsive to the needs of the children. These authors were certainly aware that, in spite of the over-reaction to Sputnik, science-oriented education was not all that was needed. For them, human-oriented education was also vitally needed; the confluent model provided them with a good starting point.

The Values Clarification Model

At the same time, another group of educators was beginning to emphasize the importance of caring, of learning to value, and of being aware of individual feelings as well as the feelings of others. This group initiated the techniques of values clarification. Perhaps this was the natural evolution of an idea whose time had come. The taxonomy of the affective domain described the categories of "receiving (attending), responding, valuing, organization, characterization by value or a value complex" (Krathwohl et al., p. 10). Raths, Harmin, and Simon (1966) designed both a learning philosophy based on the importance of valuing and a set of structured exercises that would help children experience their value-making capacity. They emphasized that no one was dictating which values were right or wrong; the objective was to help students learn how to identify, clarify, and articulate those values most important to them.

The values clarification movement has grown and matured in the 1970s. It has determined that there are some values that are more important than others. One of the most important is obviously the value of establishing one's own values. Once this step is taken, the importance of expressing those values to others and listening empathically to others' values without judging is discovered. Along with activities that help students practice identifying their own values, the model offers exercises that teach and reinforce good listening habits and promote the practice of giving positive support and feedback to others. This model is now being used in schools throughout the United States. It can be successfully incorporated into a number of classroom activities and subject areas (Simon, Howe, and Kirschenbaum, 1972; Harmin, Kirschenbaum, and Simon, 1973; Wells and Canfield, 1976).

Self-Awareness/Self-Esteem Models

In 1969, the appearance of two books had a tremendous impact on psychology and education. These were Frederick Perls's *Gestalt Therapy Verbatim* and Carl Rogers's *Freedom to Learn*. Representing Maslow's third force, humanistic psychology, both authors stressed the importance of learning in the immediate present. While Perls emphasized the need to learn and know one's self through one's body, senses, and feelings, Rogers stressed person-to-person interactions and the importance of openness and genuineness. Perls stressed the intrapersonal, while Rogers stressed the interpersonal aspects of learning.

Perls compared events occurring around people to the fine focusing of a camera in which the lens sees only one figure clearly; everything else around the subject is background or "field," and out of focus. He proposed that learning, as well as all other human behavior, moves through cyclical stages, beginning with awareness, through excitement and action, to contact (Perls, Hefferline, and Goodman, 1965). A person must be aware of a learning task or activity, must be excited by it, must act upon it, and must come into complete contact with it; only then is the cycle complete. Perls was concerned that people do not complete the cycle, choosing rather to ignore or bypass the possibility of action. It is vital for people to be active and for the learning materials to be designed to take on a personal relevance through active contact with them.

Rogers also considered learning an active process. He believed that no one can "teach" anybody anything. He looked upon teachers as facilitators who know how and when to give a helping hand, providing the stimulus necessary for the learning cycle to occur but who also know how and when to move out of the way of any student's independent movement through the learning cycle. As in his counseling approach, Rogers, the educator, stressed the importance of warmth, genuineness, and acceptance in the learning process.

Both authors, in fact, stressed the importance of the teacher being human at all times. For Perls, on the one hand, to be human is to be maximally aware, while Rogers, on the other hand, believed that to be human is to be a real person: "a real person . . . enters into a relationship with the learner without presenting a front or facade . . . he has a direct personal contact with the learner . . . he is *being* himself, not denying himself. He is *present* to the student" (Rogers, 1969, p. 106). Rogers differed from Perls only in his emphasis on unconditional positive regard between teacher and student. This is essential if any learning is to take place.

Gibb (1965) outlined styles of speaking that are most likely to threaten the listener. He also offered what he considered to be an opposite and more successful, supportive approach in each case. The "Johari window" (Luft, 1969) presented a visual model of the ways in which people reveal information about themselves to others and receive information about themselves from others. Both self-disclosure and feedback are designed to facilitate better ways of talking and listening to one another, better ways of sharing feelings with each other, better and more effective ways of communicating and increasing self-awareness.

Problem-Solving Models

Essentially these approaches are interpersonally focused. Perhaps the best-known model is that of Transactional Analysis. Based on the work of Eric Berne (1964), this model stresses the importance of "strokes." Beginning at birth and through early childhood, stroking takes physical forms. Strokes are nurturing hugs and kisses as well as disciplinary measures or angry touches. Later in development strokes take on symbolic, communicative forms. Thus, the recognition and messages that people give to each other have significance as positive or negative strokes. Being stroked results in the development of expectations or life positions about self and about others ("OK-ness" or "not-OK-ness") and in a pattern of internal roles or ego states (Parent, Adult, and Child). People operate from these positions and from an ever-shifting configuration of ego states. Moreover, they have the capability of organizing and delivering messages and strokes. This continuous interchange of messages or strokes makes up the world of human transactions. Such transactions can go smoothly between people or become crossed, leaving both parties with unfulfilled expectations and confused feelings. In the most extreme cases, crossed transactions occur based on ulterior motives; these are the "games people play."

Repeated early experience with certain strokes, with certain stroking patterns, and with certain transactions "write" an individual's life script. The decision regarding which script to adopt occurs early in life. The script sets the stage for human relations that are less open and less intimate than they could be. People continue to be less open and less intimate in their transactions, continue to react in set patterns, continue to be misunderstood and to misunderstand others until such time as they undergo a relearning experience, in which they explore the complexities of their decisions, scripts, and games. That people learn these life positions, scripts, and games is evident. What is important and less evident is the effect of these on any learning situation involving two or more people. The interpersonal flow of events can be both the process and the content of any learning, whether the learning takes place in a classroom or in the real world. Thus, personal styles and interpersonal strategies are the stuff of learning.

Glasser (1965, 1969) offered a model to assist in the interpersonal side of learning. The learner must first learn to describe or question his behavior. He must then determine its importance or its value in his life. A decision is then required regarding whether or not the learner wishes that behavior to continue. If the learner decides in the negative, he must learn to plan for positive changes. What is crucial in this model is that if the learner does not succeed in carrying out his plans for change, he takes complete responsibility and suffers the logical consequences. If, on the other hand, he does succeed, he takes credit for his victory. Glasser, however, emphasized the need to plan carefully in well-designed steps and stages so that success is virtually inevitable and failure highly unlikely. The planning is shared by the teacher and student or by the psychologist and client. Glasser also emphasized the continued investment and involvement of the helper when initial planned changes do not succeed.

In this same vein, the Effectiveness Training model (Gordon, 1975) was designed to help people identify and deal with interpersonal difficulties or problems. Two different techniques (i.e., active listening and confronting) are developed for use when another owns the problem or the self owns the problem, respectively. In addition to spelling out techniques to use with the problems, the model also clearly provides information on what approaches (i.e., "the dirty dozen"; see chapter 7) need to be avoided in such situations.

The work of Watzlawick, Weakland, and Fisch (1974) was primarily concerned with change. Their theory of learning was based on the study of natural phenomena and spontaneity, in the study of the persistence of change in the world. It stressed the use of paradoxical restructuring or "reframing" of problem situations so that undesirable behavior patterns can be appropriately and successfully modified. Understanding the intricacies of change and paradox opens a whole new range of possible techniques that can be of use in a learning situation where people are caught in repetitive and unproductive behavior patterns. Here again learning occurs in an interactional context. This model differs from others in the use of the paradox by "teachers," people other than the person who has the learning need or problem. Indeed, its view of learning might well provide a conceptual superstructure for the other problem-solving models.

The Group Dynamics Model

In a sense, much of learning and much of what has been discussed above occurs in groups and is part of the area of group dynamics. People live in and experience groups throughout their lives. Angyal (1941) described two basic processes that encompass a great deal of human experience: autonomy and homonomy. The former relates to control over one's life, a sense of power, the ability to have an impact on one's surroundings. The latter relates to belonging to some group, being dependent on others in some situations. That human beings are not loners is evident. Indeed, Bion (1961) called people "herding" animals. Something within each individual needs at least someone else, a significant other in one's life. In their development and learning, people experience both of these complex and multifaceted processes. Many times the two conflict, causing problems in intrapersonal experiences, interpersonal relations, and group relationships.

That much of learning goes on in groups is also evident. Each group has unique characteristics as well as characteristics shared by all groups. Thus, a knowledge of "groupness" or of group processes is vital to educators. The success or failure of an individual while dealing with groups either from without or from within determines in part how well he learns and how well he teaches. Much of the material in group dynamics (Cartwright and Zander, 1968) has been extrapolated and developed for practical use in the classroom (Schmuck and Schmuck, 1975). These applications are vital for any learning-oriented situation, indeed for any learning experience, whether in schools or in the real world.

Other Models and Fringe Groups

A number of other models exist that might cross an invisible line, becoming somewhat questionable. On the surface, many appear to take into consideration a person's individuality and autonomy. At first glance they may seem to offer self-actualization potential. Yet they may also provide the unwary individual with experiences and problems for which she has not bargained and for which she may be unprepared. A small number of people appear to have adopted philosophies and behaviors based on a number of these change strategies (i.e., est, Arica, and Rolfing). Mention of them here does not indicate approval or disapproval; they are merely listed with a cautionary note. Whether such models are good or bad is not to be decided here. What is important is that although they do not have a tremendous, direct impact on education, these groups may have an indirect influence on schools, citizens, and parents. Their provocativeness may allow people to become overly cautious regarding affective humanistic education. These fringe groups are the ones that are most visible and are viewed not only as part of, but also as indicative of the humanistic movement. In some organizations or educational institutions, strong opposition to allowing any affective education strategy to be implemented may result from experiences, unpleasant or threatening, with one or more of these groups.

What then do these areas have in common? From the perspective of this book, a concern with conditions that foster and facilitate individual growth and self-actualization. Self-actualization reaches back to the days of the early Greeks. It has also, more recently, been integrated into the thinking of a great many philosophers and psychologists.

> The concept of self-actualization has its earliest philosophical roots in Aristotle's doctrine of entelechy, according to which every individual being needs to realize his or her own *telos* or goal . . . the concept of self-realization lies at the heart of . . . John Dewey's ethic of potentiality and of the thoughts of such varied psychologists and psychoanalysts as Rollo May, Carl Rogers, Meddard Boss, Erich Fromm, Karen Horney and Abraham Maslow. [Friedman, 1976, pp. 5–6]

The dangers and pitfalls of self-actualization have also been evident since its early days. For many, to be self-actualized means to be extremely introverted, self-centered—"selfish." To these people, autonomy is the absolute goal. For others, homonomy becomes the most important. Yet to be truly self-actualized (the ultimate goal of all education) means neither to be selfish nor selfless. Indeed, it requires a fine balance between these. Self-actualization is difficult to achieve. The more self-centered the searching becomes, the more people seek to find out who they are, the less likely they are to find their special place, their niche in harmonious society. Jesus said, "He who would find his life must lose it." Reaching out to others, hearing their needs, and acting upon them helps people realize their full potential as people, and the greatest link people have is through communication. As imperfect as communication is, it is the most vital way to bridge the gap between ourselves and others, the most important tool to help in the great journey toward self-actualization and interdependence. Sometimes it seems as if people may never learn to communicate successfully.

> Speech flowers
> As the daisy
> Snags as the rambler rose,
> Climbing walls
> Strangles as the honeysuckle,
> Hanging over fences,
> Rampant, uncontrolled.
> The gardener has grown deaf
> And old.
>
> —Powell

Writing a few lines of verse is one way of dealing with discouraging or confusing communication, but there are more practical activities that will help to improve human interactions. The reader is invited to consider the options offered in the following chapters.

References

Angyal, Andras. *Foundations for a science of personality.* New York: Commonwealth Fund, 1941.

Berne, Eric. *Games people play.* New York: Grove Press, 1964.

Bion, Wilfred R. *Experiences in groups.* New York: Basic Books, 1961.

Bloom, Benjamin Samuel, Engelhart, Max D., Furst, Edward J., Hill, Walker H., and Krathwohl, David R. *Taxonomy of educational objectives.* Handbook I, *Cognitive domain.* New York: David McKay, 1956.

Brown, George Isaac. *Human teaching for human learning: An introduction to confluent learning.* New York: Viking Press, 1971.

Bruner, Jerome. *The process of education.* Cambridge, Mass.: Harvard University Press, 1960.

Cartwright, Dorwin, and Zander, Alvin. *Group dynamics: Research and theory.* New York: Harper & Row, 1968.

Friedman, Maurice. Aiming at the self: The paradox of encounter and the human potential movement. *Journal of Humanistic Psychology,* 1976, *16,* 5–6.

Gibb, Jack. Defensive communication. *Etc.: A Review of General Semantics.* 1965, *22,* 221–29.

Glasser, William. *Reality therapy.* New York: Harper & Row, 1965.

———. *Schools without failure.* New York: Harper & Row, 1969.

Gordon, Thomas. *Teacher effectiveness training.* New York: Peter Wyden, 1975.

Harmin, Merrill, Kirschenbaum, Howard, and Simon, Sidney B. *Clarifying values through subject matter.* Minneapolis: Winston Press, 1973.

Herndon, James. *Way it spozed to be.* New York: Simon & Schuster, 1972.

Holt, John. *Freedom and beyond.* New York: Dell, 1972.

————. *How children fail.* New York: Pitman, 1964.

————. *How children learn.* New York: Dell, 1967.

Illich, Ivan. *Deschooling society.* New York: Harper & Row, 1971.

Jacob, Philip E. *Changing values in college.* New York: Harper & Row, 1957.

Jones, Richard M. *Fantasy and feeling in education.* New York: New York University Press, 1968.

Kirschenbaum, Howard. Clarifying values clarification: Some theoretical issues and a review of research. *Group and Organization Studies,* 1976, *1,* 99–116.

Kozol, Jonathan. *Death at an early age.* Boston: Houghton Mifflin, 1967.

————. *The night is dark and I am far from home.* Boston: Houghton Mifflin, 1975.

Krathwohl, David R., Bloom, Benjamin Samuel, and Masia, Bertram B. *Taxonomy of educational objectives:* Handbook II, *Affective domain.* New York: David McKay, 1964.

Luft, Joseph. *Of human interaction.* Palo Alto, Calif.: Mayfield Publishing Co., 1969.

Ornstein, Robert E. *The psychology of consciousness.* New York: Viking Press, 1972.

Perls, Frederick. *Gestalt therapy verbatim.* Moab, Utah: Real People Press, 1969.

————, Hefferline, Ralph F., and Goodman, Paul. *Gestalt therapy: Excitement and growth in the human personality.* New York: Dell, 1965.

Raths, Louis E., Harmin, Merrill, and Simon, Sidney. *Values and teaching.* Columbus, Ohio: Charles E. Merrill, 1966.

Rogers, Carl. *Freedom to learn.* Columbus, Ohio: Charles E. Merrill, 1969.

————. The interpersonal relationship in the facilitation of learning. In D. A. Read and Sidney B. Simon (eds.), *Humanistic education sourcebook,* 3–19. Englewood Cliffs, N.J.: Prentice-Hall, 1975.

Samples, Bob. *The metaphoric mind.* Reading, Mass.: Addison-Wesley Publishing Co., 1976.

Schmuck, Richard A., and Schmuck, Patricia A. *Group processes in the classroom.* Dubuque, Iowa: W. C. Brown, 1975.

Simon, Sidney B., Howe, Leland W., and Kirschenbaum, Howard. *Values clarification: A handbook of practical strategies for teachers.* New York: Hart, 1972.

Watzlawick, Paul, Weakland, John H., and Fisch, Richard. *Change: Principles of problem formation and problem resolution.* New York: Norton, 1974.

Wells, Harold C., and Canfield, Jack. *100 ways to enhance self-concept in the classroom: A handbook for teachers and parents.* Englewood Cliffs, N.J.: Prentice-Hall, 1976.

2

People and Libraries

Answering the "Whats" and "So-Whats" about Humanistic Librarianship

The Scene: A large committee of concerned librarians, appointed by the governor of their state, is meeting to determine whether there is, in fact, a need to improve present state-wide library services. The governor has suggested to the committee that after gathering data, if necessary, the members may wish to present to the state legislature a bill that could help to correct any noted deficiencies. The group, which has been provided federal funds by the state library, conducts several surveys using professional research agencies. The results are not surprising. The state has some serious problems providing library services. One of the major difficulties is financial in nature. Geographically the state is large with a sparse, scattered population. The surveys reveal that many people do not have access to books and other materials from libraries. Others, even though libraries are close by, have not been using them frequently or even at all. A lack of information about what services are available seems to be only part of the problem.

Based on the evidence, the committee decides that legislation is indeed in order. The members begin the task of studying bills and laws that are available from various states where similar problems exist. The group thinks that it is logical that there should be, for instance, a way to have some kind of regional, cooperative network and some kind of library commission to oversee the regional network. The most important goal would be to provide equal access to library services around the state. In short, a method of sharing should be established to provide the most amount of service for the most number of people for the fewest tax dollars. With this in mind the group begins the arduous task of drawing up a bill to meet the identified needs.

And arduous it will be. For the task will involve more than clear-cut formalities; it will also involve the interactions of people. For example, in the initial stages, before the governor even appoints the members of the committee, there will be a certain amount of quiet— and some not so quiet—maneuvering on the part of people who want to become members of the group. A number of influential people representing library associations will automatically make the list. Aggressive new leaders, some popular with the powers-that-be and some not so popular, will do what they can to be added to the committee. Other people will work to prevent some individuals from being appointed.

A slice of life. No different from what happens politically everywhere. To be taken for granted, accepted as inevitable and therefore not worthy of discussion here? Not so. For what follows, also a slice of life, will work with these events to have a cumulative effect that will influence the outcome of committee business. Some people, for instance, will harbor ill feelings because they have not been chosen to work on the committee. They will work against the committee's plans, rationalizing their reasons for doing so.

On the inside of the committee there will inevitably be a struggle until one or more of the members establishes some sort of leadership role. The titular leader appointed by the governor or one elected by the members may try unsuccessfully to direct the group's activities. An executive secretary may vie for power with other people in the group and create more difficulties. Feelings of conflict may arise among representatives of separate library groups concerning the focus of legislation. Should the bill be designed to fund public library programs exclusively? After all, they have received little from the federal or the state governments in comparison to the wealth provided school libraries by the Elementary and Secondary Education Act's various titles. Should audiovisual and other media services be included as part of a state-wide program? Should these be housed in the State Library or in regional libraries? Should the State Library take a leadership role in introducing multimedia services to public libraries or should it maintain a strict print orientation? Should funding be available for public relations projects or out-reach programs for individual libraries, or should the State Library or the regional leaders provide coordinated workshops, materials, and programs? And so on.

Behind all of this will be the vested interests and the struggles of various individuals who wish to gain a foothold for their own region or their own library. As they see the bill developing, they will attempt to engineer ways to get a slice of the pie. Some will be thinking "program" and some will be thinking "power." If they can manage to have their libraries designated a regional center, they will not only have more funds but will also climb up another step in the ladder of the state hierarchy. If they can become members of this future library commission they are now designing, they will have some control not only over their own library but also over others as well. Whether all that they seek to accomplish is approached in an ethical fashion will remain to the reader's imagination, or to her memory of past experience with groups of this nature.

The facts remain. There are ways to work successfully in groups, to fulfill one's own need for professional growth and to succeed at improving the library programs without sacrificing one's integrity and without alienating one's colleagues. There are ways to effect change within a group without putting its members on the defensive. An individual librarian with some training who understands some group dynamics can change the climate of a meeting for the better, can help members to participate more successfully and to contribute to the total effort. One person can make a difference.

An extrapolation from the example of a select group of librarians working for state legislation to the individual librarian who must operate within (or deal with) committees on various levels will illustrate how broad these implications can be for the professional librarian. In addition to understanding the problems associated with group dynamics, however, librarians have some rather specific problems that have been generated throughout the history of their profession. They have been trained in the philosophy of the "science" or "service," whichever one prefers, but have of necessity become tangled with some of the issues described above, issues that further complicate matters. Some selected examples will be discussed here.

Library science, as the reader well knows, has its own special time line. Since librarians are undoubtedly familiar with the history of libraries, that history will be mentioned only in connection with a few of the factors that have created problems either within the profession or between the profession and its public.

Problem No. 1

From the days when monks were assigned (or assigned themselves) the task of copying and housing priceless manuscripts, there has been a legitimate concern for the preservation of recorded knowledge. The sharing of recorded knowledge on a wide scale could not become a practical reality until after Gutenberg's invention had evolved into a more economical press for widespread use. Even lending libraries, when first initiated, were obviously for the privileged few. It was not what a person knew, but who she knew that provided access to the precious written word. Semiprivate libraries slowly evolved, perhaps through rather democratic feelings of guilt. Next arrived Andrew Carnegie and the great leap forward. Somehow, although libraries eventually were designated "public," the public still had problems using them. Even today some kind of exclusivity lingers.

Librarians have unfortunately, and unfairly, become known as the protectors of the collection rather than as the lenders of the books, the providers of information. In addition, there have been a number of librarians who cherished the peace and solitude of the seldom-used special collection or of the research library, or who unconsciously chose cataloging as an "escape" from people. Just enough of these librarians have been mistakenly assigned to the circulation desk, the reader's advisory service, or the reference room to keep a rather unfortunate stereotype alive.

Part of the question, then, involves erasing this image once and for all and preventing it from recurring. Other questions are also important. How does an administrator learn to hire the right person for the right job? And what of those still on the job who have difficulty dealing with other human beings? Clearly a comfortable niche must be found for these people, one where their presence will not threaten other people and where they can be most helpful to the library.

Problem No. 2

Skipping down the time line to relatively modern library history brings the advent of school libraries. When special services for school children began to be organized and housed in places separate from the public library, a whole new series of "people problems" were triggered that caused tension not only between public and school librarians, but also between school librarians and the relative newcomers dealing in audiovisual technology.

To begin with, the logical course of action (i.e., placing library books and other materials in the school) seemed in some cases to seriously detract from the public library program. Children and young adults might completely forget about the public library. This sometimes proved to be the case and difficulties between formerly cooperative colleagues erupted. In addition, when audiovisual experts were asked to join with school librarians under a single program, more difficulties arose. Conflict over who was qualified to administer a combined program created more tension. Librarians lacked knowledge of audiovisual affairs and audiovisual experts lacked expertise in library science. Too often there was a shotgun wedding of sorts in which two or more people were forced to work together in spite of differing philosophies and differing educational backgrounds. One would be chosen as "top dog" and the other would be left growling in the background.

These problems did not confine themselves to individual public and school libraries with media centers, but also proliferated on the state, regional, and national levels, at which point some professional associations took up the cudgels. They also took to grinding their teeth and snarling even while masking those activities as smiles. The struggle, of course, continues today, but on a more civilized level.

Problem No. 3

Not too far removed but somewhat more futuristic in outlook is the problem that accompanies the possible evolution of libraries and media centers into more sophisticated information/computer centers. Most people have not yet come to terms with the issue of humanity versus "the machine" and with the difficulties of cybernetics as it is associated with the future of library service and librarianship as a career. Needless to say, this is not a simple extension of audiovisual services, but rather a highly specialized field of communications in itself, requiring not only additional technical expertise but also some careful philosophical thought leading to a set of values and attitudes that are compatible with human needs.

These, then, are a sampling of some of the people problems currently besetting library service. Some are directly related to a lack of understanding of human interactions, and some are related to an over-emphasis on practical work. Not too long ago, for example, an excerpt from a new book on library administration was featured in one of the library journals. The author, then director of a library school, posed theoretical problems confronting the administrator of a large public library and offered solutions on ways to handle staff problems. The majority of letters (including one from one of the present authors) published in the next two issues featured angry reactions to the clever but callous prescriptions offered by the author. There was a great deal of criticism concerning the author's lack of compassion; for example, his deliberate put-down of married women librarians who were absent to take care of a sick child. He considered such women to be detrimental factors, handicaps to the continuity of a library program and nothing more. Not only what he said, but also how he said it exemplified how mechanistic, how unaware of the human aspects of their work, library professors and librarians themselves can become. In the name of service to people, people are often forgotten.

For those who look at personnel as people with feelings, rather than as part of a strategy or game plan in library administration, there is bound to be some lack of empathy for that author's point of view. One woman in particular was unique in her reaction, since an experience she had had with the author still colored her view of the man. Only a few years before, as a young married woman finishing her library science training, she had been a student under his direction. Ill during her first and unexpected pregnancy, she had requested, on her doctor's advice, a postponement of a two-week assignment. She had been flatly refused, even though other professionals directly in charge of that part of her training were most willing to allow a change in scheduling the work. The professor's words were: "Either you do this work now or you don't graduate!" No compromise—no compassion—just finality. He never found out that the people supervising those two weeks frequently sent her to bed so that she could avoid hospitalization. They also gave her a fine evaluation, not reporting the hours she spent in bed. She graduated. How wrong to have had to proceed underhandedly! How much more complete and more rewarding her learning would have been had she been feeling well enough to participate fully. How much better all involved would have felt, had the professor been more empathic and caring.

Perhaps some might consider such a dramatic example unnecessary to highlight the librarian's professional problems. In describing the various problems with which librarians have had to deal in terms of their peoplework, it becomes obvious that in the majority of cases the metaproblem is communications. For librarians and media specialists alike the word *communication* frequently seems attached only to the type of work done in the library. The word is used in connection with that other favorite of the profession, *media*. Librarians are supposed to be experts in one field of communication, since they are, after all, specialists in delivery and retrieval of information. They are taught to establish evaluative criteria for use in the selection of all kinds of communications and examine with care the media and its relationship to the message. But their training in terms of messages has been linear and cognitive in direction. As librarians deal daily with delivery and retrieval of information, they use their intellectual expertise with pride.

And rightly so. Yet like others in education, librarians have only incidental knowledge of the affective domain—the feelings, attitudes, and values that directly affect all communication. They have not yet recognized that it carries a message beyond its content. To paraphrase Marshall McLuhan, the medium is not really the message—we are. At present the librarian's working knowledge of humanistic communication in relation to the profession is practically nil. Most librarians recognize the need to be polite, kind when possible, and diplomatic in their dealings with everyone. Most consider common sense and courtesy to be guiding forces.

The success of a library or media center program, however, depends not just upon living up to all of those national and state guidelines, all of those suggestions and orders for service on the local level; not just upon numbers of carefully selected, appropriately used media; not just upon professionally executed classification and cataloging of materials. Librarians need something more. Lasting success demands that librarians be sensitive senders and receivers of messages, positive forces for understanding and for learning. There is an infinite number of situations in library work where a knowledge of librarianship alone will offer answers to problems, but where knowledge alone is ineffective. Equally important is sensitive communication. Some illustrative situations follow.

Where, for instance, does a librarian now turn if advice is needed on how to overcome the resistance of administrators or board members when a new service is desired, or an old one needs revamping? What special skills must be possessed to deal with a personality conflict between two members of the staff? How can staff meetings that have gone stale be turned around to change them into the productive meetings they were once before? What is the best course of action to take with the disturbed person who frequents the library and obviously needs help? How should the person who needs information on an embarrassing subject, one who finds it difficult, if not impossible, to express her needs, be assisted? How should the librarian deal with the committee of moral "Minute Men" who inspect the shelves, or with the well-meaning person who wants to donate 100 books that promote her particular religious sect? How should the librarian deal on a large scale with people hostile to the library? How does the librarian dispel the negative attitude that libraries are for scholars only or that librarians are unfriendly and uncooperative people? How can librarians make peace within the various related professional groups and end the unnecessary and counterproductive divisiveness between print-oriented librarians and the audiovisual professionals? How, indeed, are librarians to understand that they should concern themselves with feelings, the messages behind the message, when their job description says nothing at all about such concerns? If librarians have survived all of these years without emphasizing humanistic values, without considering affective goals, why should they begin now?

Perhaps librarians could convince themselves of the need for training in affective communication skills by acknowledging that previous professional survival has been at a minimal level with too many paltry budgets, too many favored goals ignored, too many priorities shoved to the bottom of local, state, or federal lists. Recognition of the fact that many librarians receive low salaries, reflecting the diminished status that low-paying jobs have in this culture, may be indicative. All of these could be attributed to a lack of skills in and a lack of understanding of how to make the needs and desires of librarians appreciated and acted upon.

To convince librarians that this is not just another fad, another phase of innovation enthusiastically adopted by other educators that will pass shortly, calls for a little reading and a little research on the subject of affective education. *Fantasy and Feeling in Education* by Richard M. Jones (New York: New York University Press, 1968), *The Metaphoric Mind* by Bob Samples (Reading, Mass.: Addison-Wesley, 1976), and *Humanistic Education Sourcebook*, edited by Donald A. Reed and Sidney B. Simon (Englewood Cliffs, N.J.: Prentice-Hall, 1975) show that educators have been concerned about the affective domain, the activities of the right hemisphere of the brain, and both areas in relation to learning for some time now. Of course, all library problems are not directly traceable to poor communications or to poor public relations, but the subject of this book is peoplework (i.e., the interpersonal and group interactions that affect the success of library work). The authors will not attempt to deal with other causes of difficulties within the library except to say that those causes are often related directly or indirectly to poor communications. To put it another way, communications might be compared with the yeast that goes into making bread. The success of baking bread is related to the use of yeast, and the response of the yeast to the person who uses it is closely bound up with the other ingredients, the temperature, and even other environmental factors such as altitude—all will affect the yeast's performance. Whether the bread rises depends on many factors, but without the yeast the other ingredients are not going to make good bread. The yeast, like communication, is an essential and necessary part of what goes on. How it is handled makes the difference. The yeast, then, is to bread as communication is to library programs.

But the real reason all librarians should become more skilled and knowledgeable in affective and humanistic approaches to library/media work is precisely because they are whole human beings whose feelings, values, and attitudes do count as part of themselves and their work. Their humanity in their work, not the media, is their most important message. Librarians need validation for what they do. And they need to be able to validate others, to make contact in caring ways with the people with whom they work and the people they serve.

There are some very basic assumptions incorporated into the thinking of respected psychologists and psychiatrists that support a holistic approach to communication skills. Learning to incorporate humanistic skills in library work does not impinge upon the work of psychologists or psychiatrists; it merely simplifies their work, possibly preventing their having to intervene where healthy and skillful communication could take care of most situations or problems. There is a body of knowledge accompanied by transferable skills that can be learned to help people communicate more successfully. This knowledge and these skills are not jealously guarded by psychologists and psychiatrists; in fact, most encourage people to study and to learn the skills. If librarians continue to shun the affective domain in their work, if they claim they have no right to concern themselves with peoples' values and attitudes, they are by default dealing randomly and ignorantly with those feelings and attitudes. They are setting an example that says they do not care, they are not concerned. And thus they are less than they are capable of becoming, both professionally and humanly.

Like other educators, librarians model their values. They are involved whether they wish to be or not; they project their attitudes to the public, which interprets intuitively how it feels about them. People choose; they are not puppets. If the skills needed are not taught in approved library/ media programs and graduate schools, and if presently there is little emphasis placed on this kind of knowledge, are these circumstances to be used as librarians' excuses for doing nothing to help themselves? They may assume, as so many have before, that Psychology 101, Educational Psychology, or any other similar elective squeezed into a college or graduate school program is sufficient for most needs. But Psychology 101 is rightly reputed to be a general introduction to all kinds of psychology and Educational Psychology is, in many cases, directed toward behavioristic techniques with an emphasis on how to establish and maintain control of classroom behavior. Neither of these two courses considers the special implications of group and interpersonal dynamics as related to libraries and media centers.

Perhaps librarians will decide to help themselves. Their very philosophy encourages others to continue their learning through the use of libraries and media; they should certainly know that people do not have to sit in classrooms to learn. Mental health centers where workshops are offered are located in most areas. These are often designed for special interest groups, from business executives to police officers. Psychologists working in schools willingly offer in-service courses to interested faculty groups and counseling or consultation to individuals. Needless to say, many excellent books and audiovisual aids are available, in addition to the ones mentioned above, that offer some of the many models for humanistic problem solving.

Not too long ago, one of the authors was present at a group brought together by a friend who wished to introduce certain people working in human services. They came from many agencies in the city. The people she met were friendly, articulate, and caring. They were inspiring to talk with. Learning more about their special contributions to various programs and services gave her great hope for the children and young people involved in their programs. But something stuck in her mind; these people served, for the most part, as what one of them, a psychologist, had labeled "paid friends"; they received a fee to do things for people that good friends should be able to do for each other. If for no other reason than to prevent the necessity of such an extreme, people should improve their friendship skills. Those in library/media work should not forget how important their personalities are, how they project their messages about the importance of friendship, caring, and concern for their fellow human beings.

People take for granted their needs to learn reading, writing, and computational skills. They take pride in intellectual knowledge and cultural accomplishments. Schools, libraries, and media centers work toward helping children and adults reach their potential in these areas. Yet all grow up assuming that the caring skills will take care of themselves. Most people assume that common sense will solve any people problems. And yet common sense can be dangerous: what is common to one may not be common to another; what is sensible to one may not be at all sensible to another. In short, there may be no such thing as common sense. Look at the ordinary things that go wrong during the course of an ordinary day, the snags in understanding, the misinterpretations of words spoken, or the deliberately unkind or unheeding responses of people. Watching the sadness and violence in the evening news indicates that something is dreadfully wrong. People do not hear each other. They do not know how to listen empathically. Usually when someone is talking, others are already framing their answers inside; waiting, patiently or impatiently, for the speaker to finish so that they can offer what is in their mind. Instinctive response? Learned, not instinctive. People could relearn so that listening becomes an active response to another person's needs. A simple way to determine how intricately listening is interwoven within the practical everyday aspects of a library program has the individual check her own listening responses to see if there is any real awareness of how the other person feels as he or she speaks. Librarians, dealing with media, can begin to ask not only such questions as, "Were the needed services delivered well technically?" but also, "How did the people or person served feel about how the services were delivered?" And having asked, librarians must then listen, must actively pursue the answer. This might be called a technique of humanistic librarianship. For this profession to be considered humanistic, however, librarians must first be highly versed in asking the right questions and listening carefully to the answers before acting upon them. Then and only then may they add a new dimension to their services and justify their raison d'être with greater joy.

The whole area of feelings is a difficult one to talk about. The subjective style of this chapter, the use of certain words in it, will stimulate many different reactions. One response might hold that personal feelings have nothing to do with a person's professional life. Yet, paradoxically, readers may discount or dismiss what is written here precisely because of their own personal feelings, from anger or frustrations, not consciously recognized. Until everyone learns to deal more freely with their personal reactions, they will be only half-involved, only half-aware of the possibilities for developments within the profession.

The point of this chapter, then, is not to produce divisive feelings, but to help librarians look at their feelings and the effect these feelings have on their professional lives. It is an invitation to begin a productive dialogue on ways to join the science of their work with their artistic, creative, and intuitive selves. A confluent approach to librarianship, one that embraces an understanding of both technical expertise and humanistic skills and knowledge, is possible. It is all right for librarians to express feelings about their work and about the people with whom they work. That they should do so in an enlightened way is essential not only for their own professional survival, but also for the future of the library and information sciences.

AN EXERCISE

The Approachability Factor

The following questions are for individual use by librarians or media specialists. They can also be used as a stimulus for discussion at staff meetings or professional meetings of librarians and media specialists. The questions will help librarians check their personal involvement in their library work, their own boundary lines, their territorial feelings, and their sense of status and role. They will help librarians begin looking at the affective dimensions that underlie all that goes on in library work. Some may seem more direct than others, more pertinent to one's own job. But answer them anyway. How an individual reacts subjectively to these questions is important and will provide a clue about whether the peoplework in the library program is all it could be. If an individual becomes angry, annoyed, or in some other way upset while responding to the questions, the questions may be more on target than first realized. Examine the answers to find any rationalizations; these may indicate an attempt to protect oneself from knowledge of self or of others that could be painful. If this is the case, delay answering the questions until the whole book has been completed. In either case the questions will be discussed at other points in the book; they are, in a very real sense, what this book is about.

1. Who approaches me for help? What are my feelings that affect whether a particular individual will get more or less attention from me? (An interesting way to compile data or evidence of your choices is to keep a log for one day or one week, timing each project, each meeting, or each interaction with individuals and adding comments about the success of each experience.)

2. In what ways do I perceive the individuals who use the library? The groups? How do I weigh the individual person's needs in comparison to the needs of a larger group? What kinds of generalizations, labels, etc., do I use when speaking or thinking about the people who use the library? What percentage of my generalizations are positive? Negative? Neutral?

3. What kinds of feelings do I have towards my colleagues? How do these feelings affect our working relationship? Am I considered friendly? Approachable? Busy? Difficult to talk with? How do I check my perceptions of what people feel about me? How do they check their perceptions of me?

4. What percentage of persons who use my services, my department, do I know by name? What percentage of these people know me by name? Do I consider it important to make a conscious effort to call people by name whenever possible?

5. What percentage of the community (school, town, or other) uses the library/media center? How do I feel about using public relations and other ways of encouraging people to take advantage of my services and of the services of the library/media center? What

priority does public relations receive in the overall goals of the library program?

6. How do I feel about the criteria for evaluation of professional performance used in my library/media center? How do I feel about the people who do the evaluating? How do I evaluate myself? Are there any criteria for measuring the importance of the human relationships that are part of the professional work? Should there be? Why/why not?

7. How do any or all of my answers to the above questions affect the success or failure of the library/media center program?

In thinking about the responses in each case, ask additional questions along these lines: Can I describe my behavior accurately? Can I describe my feelings accurately? Do I wish to change in either case? If so, what can I do about it?

3 The Drive to Mastery

Exploring the "Whys" and
"Why-Nots" of Behavior

The Scene: A large, open, well-lighted conference room at a comfortable old resort hotel. Ninety librarians, from universities, schools, and public libraries, are attending a state library association meeting. The one-day program consists of a series of presentations and/or experiential activities on important and relevant topics in library service. A planning team of eight librarians meeting with four consultants (one each from the three library areas represented and a psychologist) has been charged with structuring and organizing additional presentations. Of the numerous topics available one, from their perspective, is most important. This is the teaching of library skills. Having their own ideas and input from their colleagues about how to teach this, the planning team quickly tells the four consultants that motivation is the crucial topic in the teaching of such skills. Indeed, they claim, if librarians understood motivation, it would be "ninety percent of the battle!" Moreover, as a psychologist, shouldn't one of the consultants be able to teach librarians how to motivate people to learn library skills? There is clearly a challenge to develop a supplemental session on motivation. That challenge is answered.

In the early afternoon, thirty-two participants who have selected this subtopic gather with the consultants, and the session on motivation begins. The psychologist asks the participants to generate lists of what they consider motivation to be. He posts their thoughts. They include:

grades, rewards, meeting another's expectations, drive, incentive, extra time to do something one likes, moving on to bigger and better things, finishing school, special privileges, and so forth. The psychologist, then, leads the participants through the following guided fantasy. (The reader might attempt to experience this fantasy also.) "Sit comfortably, close your eyes, and relax. In your own time, when you feel comfortable, let yourself drift backward in time. Drift backward to a point in your life when you were highly motivated to learn. Imagine that time. Imagine the situation. Who, other than yourself, was involved in this learning experience? Picture yourself and these others in your mind. What did you say to yourself or do to motivate yourself initially? What did you say to yourself or do to keep yourself motivated? What did others do to contribute to your motivation? What did they say or do to help you become motivated or help you maintain a high level of motivation? How did you feel while you were motivated? How did you feel when you accomplished the learning in question? How did the others feel? What was your reward for such learnings? What was rewarding for the other people involved? Attend to these events. Visualize them. Experience them. Explore them. Understand them as fully as you can. Now, in your own time, when you feel comfortable, let your mind drift back to the present. Reenter this room and, in your own time, when you feel comfortable, open your eyes."

The psychologist then asks the participants to list what they experienced as motivating in their fantasy. He again posts their responses. They include the following: me, self-confidence, feeling good, support from important people, feeling the job was well done, assistance in the task from another, and so forth. The remaining time in the "miniversity" session is spent comparing the lists, generating personal and group learnings, discussing changes in thinking about motivation, and discussing motivation in more general terms.

The above illustration clearly focuses on an important question that needs to be answered by all educators and librarians. Is it or is it not crucial for people in general and educators in particular to understand motivation? Teachers clearly say yes. Librarians might hedge on the response. The authors not only feel that it is crucial, but also believe that a viable concept of motivation is the single most important underpinning for learning and viewing human relations. Behavior is neither random nor capricious. Yet people spend little time trying to understand what causes others to do what they do until something unexpected, out of the ordinary, or peculiar occurs. It is the contention of the authors that everyone has experienced situations in which he has been left not comprehending why another person behaved as he did. For an example of such puzzling motivation, recently one of the authors went to a university to examine a book he hoped to include in a course. In the past the university library allowed professionals not affiliated with the school to borrow books on signature. This policy had been changed the day before the author's visit. The reason for the policy change was loss of books. In discussing the policy change, one of the librarians expressed dismay both at the loss of books and the extra paperwork the new policy would bring. And she wondered aloud about the motivation of someone who would steal a book he or she could borrow for an unlimited time.

Before turning to motivation and its relationship to general learning, a caution is in order. The material below is highly technical and somewhat difficult. It is, however, critical for all who deal with other people and/or who teach. These people must comprehend and take a stand on motivation.

Three separate lines of thought converge to highlight this book's position regarding motivation. These are: (1) the similarity of motivation for all people; (2) the actual relation of motivation to learning; and (3) the ubiquity of learning. First, a general assumption that what is motivating for one person is also necessarily motivating for all other people is apparently generally accepted. This assumption leads to a position that poses a single set of incentives or motivators. Certainly in traditional learning and work situations, motivators and incentives are similar for all involved. From the case study cited at the beginning of this chapter, motivation is seen as internal as well as external; also, many different things are listed by different people as motivating. Thus, this simple assumption is actually a complex one. Different motives can impel the same behavior; likewise, the same motives might underlie different behaviors. A quick scan of the reader's recent memory will probably provide several examples that support this complexity. The dilemma becomes clearer and more manageable if motives are separated from incentives or rewards. The former is an inner force. This single motive is similar for all people with only its outward appearance or form taking on different manifestations, as demanded by situations. It is when this point is ignored or avoided that diverse rewards and incentives (external factors) are seen not only as equivalent to motivation but also as motivation. They are, in fact, different.

Second, one important question involves motivation's relation to learning. Does learning occur only under conditions of motivation? The latent learning experiments (Tolman, 1948) demonstrated that animals not experiencing a high drive state (i.e., a condition typically associated with motivation) do indeed learn certain tasks. Two groups of rats were run through a complex maze. The first group was 24-hours hungry; the second was satiated (i.e., a condition customarily considered as providing no motive force). The number of errors and total time from start-box to goal-box were recorded for both groups. The satiated group made more errors and took a longer time to run the maze than did the hungry group, but it did the job. When the satiated group was made 24-hours hungry, however, it ran the maze with as few errors and in as short a time as the original 24-hours hungry group. Thus Tolman concluded that both groups of rats had learned the "cognitive map" of the maze. Performance, not learning, is affected by drive-state or motivation. Motivation and reinforcement, thus, are only important for performance when motivation is seen as a drive state. When viewed as an inner force, motivation existed for both the 24-hours hungry group and the satiated group. Both, after all, had learned the cognitive map.

Schachtel (1954) wrote of focal attention. This is a set of acts (attending, focusing, grasping; physical as well as cognitive) directed at objects in the real world and involves several approaches aimed at an active mental grasp of the objects. Schachtel argued that interest in such acts occurs only at times when major needs are in abeyance. Indeed, high need, high anxiety, and high drive are the enemies of focal attention, whereas low need, low anxiety, and low drive are the allies of focal attention. For example, Piaget's (1952) data indicated that an infant's exploratory experimentation occurs during periods of waking life when primary needs, distress, and anxiety seem to be exerting no pressure. Pleasure appears to be experienced as suggested by the infant's smiles, gurgles, and peals of laughter. Thus there seems to be an ever-increasing body of data that supports both Tolman's position and the contention that the child's earliest learnings (i.e., motor, cognitive, perceptual, linguistic, and social) occur in play. It is during play that the child's activity moves from random actions to actions with purpose and impact, from simple actions to more complex, patterned actions, from patterns to the object concept (i.e., that objects have substance and permanence).

Thus, during play a child's actions become progressively more organized and more purposeful. What impels this? Is it that developing organisms have a moderately strong drive to play? This is a tempting possibility. However, as further information will show, postulating a new drive is a problematic and risky option. Remember that strong drives facilitate only certain narrow learnings. They do not create conditions to allow maximum familiarity with surroundings. They are not necessary for play or for maximal contact with the environment. Breadth of learning (Bruner, Matter, and Papanek, 1955) is clearly favored by moderate and hampered by strong motivation.

In summary, a single motivational concept might be in order; also, motivation as a powerful drive appears to be necessary at best for narrow, circumscribed learnings and at worst only for performance.

The third line of thought previously mentioned holds that learning is ubiquitous. It occurs at all times and in all places. It occurs for its own sake or as a means to an end, either early or late in life. It occurs rapidly in some cases and slowly in others. One need only look around to see the number and variety of learning experiences available to people. Learning is not solely the province of, nor does it occur solely in, the school.

Current educational positions regarding motivation are in opposition to the above concepts. Witness the emphasis placed on competition, the use of grades, and the mounting resistance to attempts to remove grades. Such occur in spite of research on comparative competition, grades, and grading schemes. For example, the three major purposes of grades are: (1) to motivate students, (2) to convey information about performance, and (3) to help in administrative decision making. The work of Jonathan Warren (1971) has indicated that most grading schemes do these jobs poorly. In many cases grades motivate students only to get good grades, not to learn material. Few students are surprised by their grades; students know where they stand with respect to the materials on which they are evaluated. Although grades are widely used to select graduate students or people for jobs after graduation, they really are poor predictors of performance. Thus, what results in current educational situations is an environment that is stressful and conducive to producing high drive states. As previously noted, this type of motivation is incompatible with curiosity, experimentation, and creativity. It actually narrows the range of learning.

An increasing number of new approaches to teaching/learning are occurring in traditional school classrooms, adult community education programs, and individual reeducation experiences. From the perspective of this book they all are attempts to correct the previously noted difficulties. These newer approaches have two things in common. First, they are based on similar assumptions. These are: (1) that teachers and students are complete human beings who feel as well as think; (2) that affect and imaginal processes are as critical for learning as remembering, thinking, and problem solving; (3) that learners are unique individuals; (4) that learning is ubiquitous; and (5) that feedback is important for learning. Second, these newer approaches are compatible with a more flexible, more powerful conception of motivation. This new concept is being formulated in two very different schools of psychology, animal psychology and psychoanalytic ego psychology.

Data from Animal Psychology

Ample research evidence (e.g., Berlyne, 1950, 1955; Dashiell, 1925) has demonstrated that animals have a tendency to explore their environment. Moreover, Butler (1953, 1958), Harlow (1953), and Montgomery (1954) have shown that, in addition to their tendency to explore the environment, animals will learn tasks when the sole reward is the opportunity to explore a novel environment. One explanation of these findings points to exploration as a consequence only of secondary reinforcement; that is, that exploration must be paired with primary reinforcers (e.g., food, water, copulation) that reduce primary drives (e.g., hunger, thirst, sex). Yet the learning based on exploration was resistant to extinction even when primary reinforcement of primary drives did not take place. This clearly goes against the theories of primary and secondary reinforcement; that is, that secondary reinforcers work only for a limited time in the absence of pairing with primary reinforcers. Of more importance, the results require the assumption that primary reinforcers have to be paired with exploration. This may be the case with mature animals; young animals, however, are rewarded for following the same cues to the same responses. Movement toward novelty leads to no reward. More specifically, young animals are fed only after they experience hunger and the smells from their mothers and only after they approach the familiar mother. If they did otherwise, they would not be fed. Yet during intervals when they are satiated, they explore with no apparent primary-secondary reward links. Thus it appears that movement toward novelty is carried out for no reward, at least as primary and secondary reinforcers are most often defined as rewarding and motivating.

Another explanation of the above findings ties exploration to reduction of anxiety/fear. Montgomery and Monkman (1955), however, have demonstrated that fear induced in animals before entering a new situation did not increase exploration. In spite of the strong arguments that stimulus characteristics of novel situations might well arouse anxiety and that exploration reduces anxiety, fear and exploration are clearly incompatible.

Similar research (Harlow, 1953; Kagan and Berkun, 1954) has shown that animals have tendencies toward activity and manipulation, and that they learn tasks for the opportunity to be active and/or to manipulate objects. As with exploration, activity and manipulation have been considered secondary reinforcers. Likewise, they have been viewed as anxiety/fear reducers. Viewing activity and manipulation in these ways leads to problems similar to those encountered when exploration was so considered (i.e., learning that is resistant to extinction even without pairing with primary reinforcers and induced fear decreasing activity and manipulation). It is difficult to consider activity and manipulation as secondary reinforcers and it is more difficult to consider them as circular, anxiety reducers.

An apparent explanation of such problems is to add exploration, activity, and manipulation to the list of primary drives. Yet even this does not fully resolve the difficulties. These forms of behavior do not show the required functional properties of a drive (noted below). Specifically, they appear to be related to characteristics of the environment rather than to a *tissue deficit*. Similarly, these characteristics cannot be linked with *strong persistent stimuli*, since animals readily disregard the stimuli when weary. Likewise, they do not lead to *consummatory responses* (e.g., eating, drinking, copulating); during these activities the animals' behavior gradually subsides. Last, they as often as not lead to an increase in the drive, rather than to a decrease. This *reduction* of a drive is considered a key reinforcing property in traditional conceptions of motivation.

Changing Ideas about Motivation in Psychoanalytic Ego Psychology

One of the cornerstones upon which Freud built his psychoanalytic theory is the notion of instinct. Instincts are "somatic demands on mental life" and "the ultimate cause of all activity" (Freud, 1949, p. 20). They supply energy as powerful, persistent stimuli. The ego channels this energy into organized behavior; the goal of this behavior is to put an end to the stimuli. "The task of the nervous system is—broadly speaking—to *master stimuli*" (Freud, 1925, p. 63).

In spite of its heuristic value and parsimony, several psychoanalytic theorists have found Freud's instinct theory, with its two basic forces—sex and aggression—too limiting. Freud aimed to show how these drives could be channeled into constructive ends, but additional concepts were necessary to account for behaviors remote from instincts. Hendrick (1942) posited an additional major instinct—the instinct to master a segment of the environment. This was an inborn drive to do and to learn how to do. Accepting the instinct to master creates a dilemma. First, it does not have a somatic source external to the ego; it is an ego instinct. This goes against an important requirement of psychodynamic instinct theory—that all instincts have a somatic source or represent somatic demands. Second, there does not appear to be a sequence of painful stimulation followed by pleasurable release, a sequence typical to instinctual or to drive-induced behavior.

Fenichel (1945), in an attempt to maintain the integrity of instinct theory, argued that mastering behavior reduces anxiety. This position, for reasons similar to those given regarding animal exploration, activity, and manipulation, is not highly probable. Mastering behavior requires awareness, a broad range of skills, and an approach-oriented behavioral style. Anxiety-evoking situations impact these in a negative way. They cause a decrease in such characteristics. Because of that, to describe mastering a behavior as a way to reduce anxiety that decreases mastering skills in the first place seems circular and inadequate. One would not be hard pressed to conclude that anxiety induced in humans before entering new situations would not increase mastering. Likewise, when in new situations the induced anxiety would actually decrease mastering. New experience might indeed arouse anxiety. To argue that a set of behaviors that requires low levels of anxiety, both for development and for maintenance, also be the set of behaviors designed to reduce anxiety in new experiences again seems clearly circular and inadequate.

In a set of definitive writings on the ego, Hartmann (1950, 1958) argued for the ego as a conflict-free set of functions. He viewed the ego's task as directing energy to culturally valued events for the purpose of organizing reality. This energy is neutralized libido and aggression. This seemingly simple acceptance of the concept of neutralization is of interest and importance. Hartmann was confronted with a problem similar to the orthodox animal psychologists. He worked within the context of a limited number of somatic drives. Yet much behavior appeared impelled by external, nonsomatic forces, and it was necessary to determine the internal energy source for behaviors that were unrelated to instinctual drives. In order to account for such events, he used neutralized instinctual energy, which appears similar in form to and which suffers the same limitations as secondary reinforcement. For having accomplished its task, the neutralized ego energies should not have to continue to impel behavior. Staying within this context, he was forced to stretch his theory beyond its limits.

Kardiner and Spiegel (1947) proffered the notion of action systems to account for adaptive behavior (e.g., thinking, perceiving, learning, etc.). Integration of these functions and the more important global integration of self in the real world require repeated, successful experiences in the world. Kardiner pointed out that children are gratified when they discover a connection between a movement and its accompanying sensations. Even greater gratification is experienced when actions are successfully carried out. Similar to Mittelmann's (1954) concept of motility (i.e., the motor urge to manipulation and examination) and to Erikson's (1952) sense of industry, Kardiner's position emphasized the person as the center of purposeful, coordinated activity.

Thus, orthodox psychodynamic ego psychology is faced with a problem similar to, if not identical with, that facing animal psychology. Curiosity, intellect, and idiosyncratic interests cannot be adequately explained by psychodynamic psychology's traditional view of drives/instincts. Postulating new instincts (e.g., motility, mastery, industry) imbedded in a drive reduction framework is inadequate. Likewise, such new instincts and drives that require reduction overcomplicate an already complex issue.

Recent Views about Motivation

The common element in the situation faced by the two schools is that of the relationship between behavior and the environment. Both fall short of an adequate accounting of exploratory or experimental behavior. Both encounter difficulties in attempting to explain the organism's proclivities to manipulate, explore, and change the environment. Thus, the behaviors in question are those that have an effect on the environment. They modify the schema and the configurations of stimuli and events around the organism; they bring a degree of novelty where there was familiarity. Rogers addressed this issue (Evans, 1975). He indicated that people look for more enriched, more complicated stimuli. Motivation, then, is the basic tendency toward growth, toward maintaining and enhancing. His is a tension-induction, rather than a tension-reduction, position. Both induction and reduction produce a difference-in-sameness (Hebb, 1955) in the stimulus field. Motivated behaviors are directed toward the continual modification of stimulus cues or elements with an eye toward change and growth and toward the development of an optimal balance between the familiar and the novel.

Consider an infant. The infant's eyes follow a moving object. His hand later grasps the object. This is not random activity. Piaget clearly pointed out the infant's special interest in objects affected by his own movement. For example, Piaget noted that during the fourth month the infant's play is centered on the results he can produce. Also, the infant appears to use play to make interesting spectacles last. By the second half-year, the infant not only explores objects, but also experiments on them using a repertoire of actions and attempts to initiate results. Piaget has designated four stages of a child's approach to new objects: (1) visual exploration, (2) tactile exploration, (3) slow moving of objects in space, and (4) using the repertoire of actions (i.e., shaking, striking, swinging, etc.) to study effects produced.

To account for the trends evident in the field of motivation, White (1959) organized the observations and speculations under a single concept. Behaviors all have a singular meaningfulness when viewed as interlocking transactions between the child and the environment. The child "selects for continuous treatment those aspects of his environment which he finds it possible to affect in some way. His behavior is selective, directed, persistent—in short motivated" (White, p. 320). For White, the child is developing throughout his life an effective familiarity with his environment. He explores the environment around him, discovering what effects he has on it and what effect it has on him. "To the extent that these results are preserved by learning, they build up an increased competence in dealing with environment" (White, p. 320).

This sense of competence is directed, guided, and impelled by effectance—its motivational component. White argues for a continuous cycle, from stimulus to perception to action to effect to stimulus and so on, repeatedly. Thus, the developing child, in dealing with the environment, carries on continuous transactions that gradually change his relationship to the environment. Therefore, competence-effectance-based behavior has no consummatory climax; it is a trend, not an end. It is aroused by stimulus conditions that offer difference-in-sameness. It affects the stimulus conditions so as to produce further difference-in-sameness. It subsides when exploration renders the stimulus field without new possibility.

Competence-effectance, then, is the stuff of motivation. It and it alone makes sense out of the multitude of behaviors displayed by people. Of more importance, it is the single motivational concept that successfully lends itself to understanding all types of learning processes. It works as well with classroom learning as it does with an infant's cumulative, incidental learning. Is a student in the classroom any less likely to select aspects of his environment to impact successfully than an infant? Is he more likely to learn across a wide area under conditions of stress than his younger counterpart? Competence-effectance also works both with structured, group instruction and with self-directed, individualized learning. And it works equally as well with personal-interpersonal experiences as it does with content-curricular learning. Numbers and format do not appear to significantly affect it. It relates to an individual and his mastery alone. Individuals are compared only to their own past and future performances. Most important, it applies to learning in classrooms, to learning in libraries, as well as to learning in life. In later chapters further applications will be noted.

Impact

This exercise is best done by a trio. It can be done, however, individually. If done with two other people, take turns being the interviewee while the others help by questioning, exploring specifics, paraphrasing, and listening.

Consider all the activities, all the tasks that you do during a typical day. These can be anything you do. They can involve your work, but do not necessarily need to be limited to that. Share these with your trio-mates (or list them). Consider these. Allow yourself and your mates some time to see if your list is inclusive. Below are several questions that might be helpful.

1. Do you have any hobbies? What are they?
2. Have you included anything that relates to your family life? What are some of the typical things you are called on to do in your family?
3. Have you included things that relate to your friends? What are some of the typical things you do with or for friends?
4. Have you included all daily activities, no matter how trivial they may seem?
5. What are some thoughts you have during the day about activities that you want to learn, to experience, or to take up in the near future?
6. What types of reading do you do? How much of it relates to your work, to your hobbies, to just relaxation and pleasure?

Now that the activities are listed, go back through them and indicate: (1) which you consider fun or enjoyable; and (2) which of them are activities that you think create impact either on you or on the people and objects in the world around you. Do any affect the world in which you live? Do any stimulate you or others? Do any enhance or enrich you or others? For those that you judge as having impact, answer the following questions:

1. Where did you learn the activity?
2. How did you become interested in the activity?
3. Who, if anyone, taught you the skills involved in the activity?
4. Do you consider yourself proficient in the activity? If you do not consider yourself proficient, what additional steps do you need to take in order to become proficient? Have you made the requisite plans to take the steps to become proficient?

5. Have you convinced anyone else to engage in the activity? Have you taught anyone the activity?
6. How many of the activities that you judge as having impact can you say are also fun?

With the other members of the trio, go over all the tasks to ensure that you have not missed any that might indeed have impact. Use the interview format from above to make a comprehensive list of the transactions that you have with your day-to-day world that allow you to affect it in some way. Take some time to think about the activities and their relation to competence-effectance.

Be sure to switch and let your trio-mates do a similar listing.

References

Berlyne, Daniel Ellis. The arousal and satiation of perceptual curiosity in the rat. *Journal of Comparative and Physiological Psychology*, 1955, *48*, 238–46.

———. Novelty and curiosity as determinants of exploratory behavior. *British Journal of Psychology*, 1950, *41*, 68–80.

Bruner, Jerome S., Matter, Jean, and Papanek, Miriam Lewis. Breadth of learning as a function of drive level and mechanization. *Psychological Review*, 1955, *62*, 1–10.

Butler, Robert A. Discrimination learning by rhesus monkeys to visual-exploration motivation. *Journal of Comparative and Physiological Psychology*, 1953, *46*, 95–98.

———. Exploratory and related behavior: A new trend in animal research. *Journal of Individual Psychology*, 1958, *14*, 111–20.

Dashiell, John Frederick. A quantitative demonstration of animal drive. *Journal of Comparative Psychology*, 1925, *5*, 205–8.

Erikson, Erik H. *Childhood and society*. New York: Norton, 1952.

Evans, Richard Isadore. *Carl Rogers: The man and his ideas*. New York: E. P. Dutton, 1975.

Fenichel, Otto. *The psychoanalytic theory of neurosis*. New York: Norton, 1945.

Freud, Sigmund. Instincts and their vicissitudes. *Collected papers*. Vol. 4. London: Hogarth Press, 1925.

———. *An outline of psychoanalysis*. New York: Norton, 1949.

Harlow, Harry F. Mice, monkeys, men, and motives. *Psychological Review*, 1953, *60*, 23–32.

Hartmann, Heinz. Comments on the psychoanalytic theory of the ego. *Psychoanalytic Study of the Child*, 1950, *5*, 74–95.

———. *Ego psychology and the problem of adaptation*. New York: International Universities Press, 1958.

Hebb, Donald Olding. Drives and the C.N.S. (conceptual nervous system). *Psychological Review*, 1955, *62*, 243–54.

Hendrick, Ives. Instinct and the ego during infancy. *Psychoanalytic Quarterly*, 1942, *11*, 33–58.

Kagan, Jerome, and Berkun, Mitchell. The reward value of running activity. *Journal of Comparative and Physiological Psychology*, 1954, *47*, 108.

Kardiner, Abram, and Spiegel, Herbert X. *War stress and neurotic illness*. New York: Hoeber, 1947.

Mittelmann, Bela. Motility in infants, children, and adults. *Psychoanalytic Study of the Child*, 1954, *9*, 142–77.

Montgomery, Kay C. The role of the exploratory drive in learning. *Journal of Comparative and Physiological Psychology*, 1954, *47*, 60–64.

———, and Monkman, John A. The relation between fear and exploratory behavior. *Journal of Comparative and Physiological Psychology*, 1955, *48*, 132–36.

Piaget, Jean. *The origins of intelligence in children*. New York: International Universities Press, 1952.

Schachtel, Ernest G. The development of focal attention and the emergence of reality. *Psychiatry*, 1954, *17*, 309–24.

Tolman, Edward C. Cognitive maps in rats and men. *Psychological Review*, 1948, *55*, 189–208.

Warren, Jonathan R. *College grading practices: An overview*. Washington, D.C.: ERIC Clearinghouse on Higher Education, 1971.

White, Robert W. Motivation reconsidered: The concept of competence. *Psychological Review*, 1959, *66*, 297–333.

4

Feeling, Fantasy, and Metaphor

The Crucial Components of Confluent Education

The Scene: A media center in an excellent suburban high school. An audiovisual technician and a teacher in a program for students with special learning needs have shown a videotape, previously aired on commercial and public television, dealing with three families and their reactions to a dying family member. The tape, which is poignant and powerful, has left the learners in a state of anxiety and discomfort. One can easily imagine what some of their fantasies might be. Since one of the sequences focused on a funeral, the teacher takes funerals as a point of departure for her class discussion. She asks if any of the learners had ever attended a funeral. One youngster quickly indicates that he had. He stops short of indicating whose it was. The teacher, probing, asks whose funeral it was. He replies, "My mother's and father's!" Everyone's anxiety and discomfort increase to almost unmanageable levels. The teacher, realizing the class period is just about over, ends the session by stating, "Well, isn't that sad and interesting. Let's stop early today. Class dismissed!" She and the technician were spared further discomfort, as was the class, when the boy did not attend any session for approximately two weeks thereafter.

Several days after the incident, the teacher, talking with her colleagues in the teachers' room, tells of the experience and her embarrassment. Courageously, she admits she had no idea what she could have done differently. Her colleagues laugh and tell her that both of the student's parents are indeed alive and well. Even more chagrined, the teacher decides to let the incident pass and not to confront the youngster. Several months later, the teacher meets the youngster's mother at an open house. How complex indeed are people and the responses they make to the materials used to teach them. How complex the media, too!

Ronald Laing, in his book *The Politics of Experience* (1967) stated that few books are forgivable. Most media are unforgivable. They offer to readers, under various guises, the experiences of their authors. Not all of these experiences are comfortable or beautiful. Similarly, not all readers' reactions are positive. Indeed the written word and other media stimuli have an amazing capacity to excite many different feelings and an unending capability to generate a multitude of images. Since these feelings can range from extremely positive to overwhelmingly negative and since images can range from pleasurable to horrific, a person involved with books or other forms of media must perforce deal with thoughts, feelings and images. To do less would be at best unfair and at worst inadequate. This necessity is the crux of confluent education. Without adequate attention paid to feelings and images, thoughts alone are incomplete education. One might as well avoid thinking if one avoids feelings and fantasies.

Whether one views art, science, literature, experience, or people as the subject matter of learning, the importance of fully integrating thoughts, feelings, and fantasies will become evident. Even skeptics concede this point with regard to art and, to a lesser extent, to experience and people. But how can feelings and fantasies play a role in science and literary analysis? Is not mathematics a dispassionate process of manipulation, one requiring objective critical analysis? And what is the goal of the college sophomore if not to understand and speak eruditely about *Ulysses*? Can the phantasmagorical representations of science fiction be called literature? Would one place Lem's *Solaris*, let alone Clark's *Childhood's End* or Vonnegut's *Sirens of Titan*, in the same category with Mann's *The Magic Mountain*? Are sketchings of children and primitive man of the same quality as Michelangelo's Sistine Chapel paintings?

In spite of any personal reactions or answers, which naturally depend upon an analysis of the above, the objects mentioned as well as the observations have one thing in common. That is, they generate cognitions, emotions, and images. Any attempt either to separate intellect, affect, and imagination or to value one above the other two is artificial and misleading. Too often the exclusive reliance on objective criteria and facts is used to cast doubt on the usefulness of subjective interpretation. Hence, the quest for the one, true meaning of an Emily Dickinson poem. In addition, rigid beliefs based on an inflexible, objective, cognitive structure too often delay rich discoveries prompted by affect and fantasy. Witness the experiences of and reactions to Galileo and Darwin. Far too often objectivity and cognition have prevented discoveries and total human growth by denying affect and imagination. If educators address only one aspect of personhood or provide conditions that allow people to discredit the other aspects, they will find themselves doing only a part of what could be done. It is important to remember that children and adults are whole human beings who think, feel, and fantasize.

Apparently a growing number of educators are becoming concerned with the purely cognitive approach to learning. And rightly so. Witness a large number of students at the University of Iowa's Summer Writer's Workshop who, even with their cognitive understanding and their technical proficiency, do not succeed in writing anything of quality. Witness the incoming students at the University of Cincinnati's College of Design, Architecture, and Art who, despite high aptitude test scores, cannot master, beyond certain minimal standards, the initial wood-sculpturing task and who apparently learn to conform their creativity to the accepted criteria of their instructors (personal communication from John Peterson and Leonard M. Lansky). Listen to college professors who find that more and more freshmen have great difficulty writing a coherent essay and thinking critically. Reports indicate that in ever-increasing numbers graduating seniors from varied high schools cannot read successfully at their grade level.

Most educators feel strongly about these last two examples. The first two, however, seem to be of less concern. It is not insignificant that creative writing and art have as much to do with feeling and imagination as they do with thinking. These two processes (i.e., affect and imagery) have long been neglected by educators. When not neglected, the two processes are a source of controversy and conflict. A school system known to the authors highlights this problem. In that system the junior high language arts program is designed as two years of minicourses including film making, drama and directing, short story writing, science fiction, horror tales, and so forth. Its primary emphasis is on stimulating creativity. In many cases, little or no time is spent working on basic language arts skills. The program, then, is clearly focused on affect and on imagination. Cognition plays an important but small role. For some faculty members it is even totally ignored.

After two years, students move on to the senior high and its more traditional English program. The high school faculty members make no bones about their concern that students are poorly prepared for the senior high school's cognitive focus. This occurs despite the high school's minicourse sequence. The high school faculty will have no truck with the "nonacademic" junior high program. It not only does not prepare students for more advanced language arts skills, but also seemingly undoes what students have mastered in elementary school.

Attempts at bringing these two faculties together, which might be characterized as negotiations between sycophants on the one hand and bearers of sacred shibboleths regarding literacy on the other, have done little but polarize them. Subtle and not-so-subtle blaming and name-calling have resulted. The junior high teachers call attention to the stultifying and noncreative conditions that exist at the senior high. They also indict the elementary teachers for not doing an adequate job. The senior high teachers imply that their junior high counterparts are at best therapeutic coddlers, at worst radicals who do not value learning and thinking. Do thinking, feeling, and imagining really fit together? Can they peacefully coexist? Can a "no-lose" solution be found? Under such conditions perhaps neglect is better than conflict.

The contemporary battle cry is "back to the basics!" With more emphasis on the practice of reading, writing, and arithmetic the major problems will be corrected. After all, no one can be taught to be a writer, an artist, or to be creative. An individual is either born with talent or is not. Krathwohl, Bloom, and Masia (1964) confronted this "either-or" set when they set out to develop a taxonomy for the affective domain. This lack of concern for feeling and fantasy accounts at least in part for the long interval between these authors' two taxonomies. Jerome Bruner (an Oxford University pedagogue), although less so than before, still has doubts about whether the affective can in most curricular areas be combined with the cognitive. And here a popular media advertisement can be paraphrased: "When St. Jerome speaks, educators listen." Fortunately, at least two (i.e., Richard M. Jones and Bob Samples) did not listen. Jones, in fact, attributes the idea for his important book, *Fantasy and Feeling in Education* (1968), to a presentation by Bruner. At the Endicott Conference, Jones invited Bruner to speak to the issues that Jones had raised concerning the necessity of attending to emotions and fantasies. Bruner's eloquent presentation did everything but allow the controversy to be reopened. There clearly was no support offered by Bruner. In retrospect this turned out to be a very fortunate lack of support; it allowed Jones to set out on a journey that resulted in his book, still the definitive statement on confluent education.

For purposes of simplicity, the authors have grouped the numerous ideas, experiments, and approaches regarding confluent education into two major models. With all due respect to George Isaac Brown (1971), who coined the phrase "confluent education," these are (1) the Integrated model associated with Jones and (2) the Metaphorical model associated with Samples.

Integrated Confluence

Jones argued for an instructional process that places equal emphasis on thoughts, emotions, and images. These three distinct but interrelated processes are the cornerstones of personal and relevant learning. Although they are not one and the same, they are inextricably interwoven.

Entering the world of education through the back door as a therapeutic consultant, Jones's initial work was more therapeutic than educational. He stated:

> I have courted dreams and daydreams in classrooms, devised "pre-conscious exercises" involving darkened rooms or closed eyelids, made confidentiality pacts and other such quasi-therapeutic agreements with groups of students, have interpreted their resistances, finessed their transferences (and the corresponding counter-transferences), engaged their silences, given assignments which required autobiographical introspection, improvised examinations which elicited involvement of the "primary process," and have in other ways tried to involve emotion and fantasies in the instruction process—by *following* the therapeutic model. [Jones, pp. 82–83]

Yet difficulties with this therapeutic approach caused him to have reservations. It is not uncommon for learners to do what is asked of them; anyone who has taught realizes this. Because of this situation, in spite of the enthusiasm and willingness shown by learners, Jones questioned whether his techniques represented educational progress. Closely related to this was a suspicion that anything new, anything that relieved the deadly dull nature of classroom experiences would be greeted with enthusiasm by learners, if only because it was different. Jones acknowledged that the successful experiences occurred with college psychology students and with very young children, both of whom had some vested interest in feelings and in fantasies. Thus, the results might have suffered from a noticeable lack of generalizability. That people learn better when they are less anxious and more comfortable with themselves is well known. With this in mind, Jones was concerned that the gains in learning were only incidental, resulting from increased comfort rather than from successful instructional methodology. Teachers also manifested more than a modicum of resistance to "bootlegged psychotherapy," which they saw as part-and-parcel of his methods. Of most importance, however, was Jones's realization that the proliferation of innovative curricular materials provided teachers with the means to link thinking, feeling, and imagining. To work effectively and affectively with these new materials was not only crucial but also a way to deal with the difficulties encountered by espousing bootlegged therapy.

Even though the new curricular materials were greeted enthusiastically, the resistance remained. Only after initial evaluations demonstrated more richness and depth in student learning did resistance diminish slightly. In point of fact, resistance to affective and imaginal dimensions of learning continues. More and more educators, however, are taking the first tentative steps toward using materials and processes that generate feelings and fantasies. This is occurring in spite of their resistances, because of the ubiquity of emotions and imagination.

For Jones and for the present authors, all instruction begins by appealing to and stimulating the imagination, even in cases when this happens by chance or where it becomes discouraged because of policy or through uncertainty. Such appeals to the imagination can range from the novelties of a school to the evocative nature of the "unforgivable" media with which everyone comes into contact. Hence, it is crucial for librarians and teachers to find ways to work more systematically with imagination and with its concomitant feelings.

Perhaps the best way to show the reader the value of fantasy and imagination to the library profession is to ask him to allow himself a moment of fantasy to do the following: Imagine the ideal library, the library you could have if you could wave a magic wand and make it so. What would that library look like? How would it differ from the one in which you presently work? Would it be larger, smaller, would it have more rooms, fewer? What colors would be used? What style windows, chairs, tables, desks? What kinds of materials and services would users want? Are there possibilities for expanding services? Who would staff the library? How would the staff work together to decide what work is to be done? How would they be governed? Where would their budget come from? How large would that budget be?

These are just a few of the questions the librarian could be asked to answer that might, if allowed to reach fruition, change the course of events. To say that librarians' fantasies, their dreams and imaginings have real importance to the directions that their libraries follow is to say that inventiveness, intuition, and creativity do count for something not only in planning but in daily work. Every day in some office or at some work station in the library good ideas, possibilities for change, improvements in present operations come out of daydreams. Do not discount the multiple possibilities therein. Plan for them and encourage their inclusion wherever possible.

The authors wish to take this opportunity to dispel any potential misconceptions about imagination. Imagination is ubiquitous. For some people, however, it is more freely experienced and more easily expressed. Jones considers imagination coupled with the human capacity for symbolization to be the processes that make people distinctly human and naturally selective. That imagination is rich in young children is well documented and evident; that it decreases for too many people as a function either of maturation or of education is moot, but sad in either case.

Educators the world around profess a goal that encourages the creation of materials, methods, media, and approaches that will stimulate creative thinking. But creative thinking alone? What of creative fantasies, creative feelings? Why limit creativity to thinking alone? Might it not behoove educators to transcend their intellectual biases and utilize emotions and images with thoughts so that the totality of learning might be enriched? To work with metaphors and with imaginal reveries, to allow these to flow freely and connect with thoughts and feelings, is the stuff of creativity.

Too often, in response to the perception that such is indeed bootlegged psychotherapy, educators invoke the threats or anxieties that might be experienced by their learners as reasons to shy away from the imaginal and the affective. Yet how can they be avoided? By virtue of being whole human beings, learners experience fantasies and feelings as well as thoughts. That anxiety or threat might well occur is reason to avoid these aspects of personhood only if either is allowed to occur, recur, or grow in an unchecked fashion. Jones offered a model that does much to clarify the close relationships between anxiety and creative learning and between these two and imagination. Again, let Jones speak for himself:

These interrelations can be schematized so:

(imagination & aloneness & helplessness) = anxiety ← psychotherapy

instruction → (imagination & community & mastery) = creative
learning

[This diagram] says that imagination plus aloneness plus helplessness produces anxiety, which may be relieved by psychotherapy. And that instruction may lead to imagination plus community plus mastery, which produces creative learning. [Jones, p. 77]

A learning situation, therefore, provides the two necessary conditions, community and mastery, that can preclude anxiety in particular, and feelings in general, from reigning unchecked and leading to the need for therapeutic intervention. This occurs, for example, when the learning situation involves a librarian and a person or a teacher and a class. The former case ideally features a community of two working toward mastering an objective. The latter features a community of any number working toward mastering a concept or topic. The assumption that community is a gathering of more than two may be misleading. Everyone needs a significant other(s) in his life. People may indeed be "herding" animals as Bion suggests, but a sense of community can arise from the contact one person has when he visits the library and is treated in a friendly and cooperative manner by one person who knows his name and something about him. It is the regular contact with another known individual in familiar surroundings and happy circumstances or productive congenial circumstances that counts as a kind of community experience of value. Parenthetically, who better than the librarian knows the numberless, lonely people who frequent the library and who must deal with feelings, with fantasies, and with thoughts without the benefit of community. More specifically, if community is defined as reciprocal sharing between two or among three or more people on the cognitive, affective, and imaginal levels, one can ask whether any instructional formats make adequate use of community. The authors believe that community is frequently missing in instruction. Thus, in instructional settings there are numberless people who do not have the benefit of this vital component.

From the above it should be obvious that Jones does not argue for cultivation of feelings for feelings' sake, nor fantasies for fantasies' sake. Instruction is designed to use these processes in order to gain a mastery of one's feelings and images in concert with others and, more important, in concert with one's thoughts. This concert of feelings, fantasies, and thoughts used in conjunction with one or more "conductors" paves the way for *outsight*. Jones describes outsight as "grasping, enlivening, enhancing, discovering, making one's own this-or-that datum in the real world—by virtue of gracing it with this-or-that private image" (Jones, p. 80). He gives an example of a child who in response to a question about the meaning of infinity likens it to a box of Cream of Wheat. This is an example of outsight. What makes it important is not that it is a creative analogy, but the process by which it was developed. Jones describes that process as he deciphered it from that child. The child had a more than moderate reading problem and was given to outbursts of profanity and other obstreperous behaviors. His father had run away from the family when the boy was quite young. There quickly developed a conspiracy of silence within the family about the father. Such a silence left the child with a number of unanswered questions, with a number of nagging, painful feelings, and with a number of unchecked fantasies regarding the causes of father's leaving in general, and of his own role in the situation in particular. Often the mother, who worked to support the family, would leave the child at the breakfast table with his bowl of this hot cereal. While waiting to go off to school, he would be bored and would experience the questions, feelings, and fantasies surrounding the loss of his father. He would also sit looking at the man depicted on the box, who was holding a box with the picture of a man holding a box, and so forth. The longing for his father was indeed infinite. At some preconscious level this longing combined with his questions, feelings, and fantasies, and with the visual image of the box of Cream of Wheat. Thus, the response to the teacher's question. Interesting, to say the least.

The above example represents a crucial cyclical process that is implied in Jones's position. While he gives attention to the importance of linking preconscious thoughts, feelings, and fantasies with conscious, symbolic representations of these three, and while he talks of the ties with respect to outsight, he does not directly address this cycle of divergent-convergent operations. He does, however, indicate the importance of such a cycle when referring to Silberer's (1951) auto-symbolic phenomenon. The authors want to make these implicit references explicit. The interplay of preconscious processes (i.e., for these purposes elements just out of the consciousness) and the outward movement of thinking, feeling, and imagining are clearly divergent. They tie together, albeit loosely, elements that are both closely and remotely associated to the topic at hand. Yet it is the apparently rapid, narrowing convergence of these elements that allows certain essential links to be made and to be creatively displayed. To operate only divergently would be to create a chaotic state of consciousness without clarity or order. To function only convergently would be to create a narrow, rigid state of consciousness without room for differences. The former might be reflected in the anarchistic, disordered thinking of the schizophrenic while the latter might be reflected in the too well-ordered world of the ruminative, obsessive personality. To do both in a balanced way is to exist, experience, and learn creatively. This is reflected in the innovative classrooms and curriculum discussed so knowingly and intimately by Jones.

To highlight this position, return to the opening scene of the present chapter. What is to follow is in no way obviated by that teacher's discovery of the student's falsehood. That this example points out the potent effect of affective and imaginal qualities of a lesson is obvious. Even though this particular lesson dealt with a provocative topic, one is not hard pressed to come up with others equally affective and imaginal.

What might the teacher and the technician have done? Addressed in some detail, the incident clearly demonstrates the instructional method advocated by Jones. The teacher could have had all the learners list their feelings when the youngster shared his experience. Similarly the learners could have written their fantasies about the videotape and about their peer's information. These listings could have been posted on newsprint, on the chalkboard, or on an overhead projector. Any similarities could have been underscored, and differences could have been pointed out. Several questions could have been asked to harness the feelings and fantasies. For example, What is death? What did it mean to the people in the videotape? What does it mean to you? What does dying and death do to people associated with it? How do you suppose the people in the videotape felt? How do those feelings compare to your lists? Are they similar? Are they different? How does your list compare with your classmate's who has experienced death first hand? Are they the same? Are they different? At this point, to generalize and provide the conditions that facilitate community and mastery, the teacher could have asked derivatives of the following questions: How do people deal with and make sense out of death? Do different cultures or societies handle it in the same or in different ways? Do humans deal with death differently than other animals? How? Why?

The audiovisual technician could have compiled a list of all the available audiovisual material on death. With the help of other media center staff, she could have prepared a comprehensive set of all such materials. This material could then have been made available to learners. A complete unit on death from a biological, a psychological, a sociological, an anthropological, and a personal perspective could have been developed. This unit, then, could have been made available through the media center to other classes at this particular high school, or to classes at any number of other area high schools.

What occurred allowed images, aloneness, and helplessness to generate anxiety and avoidance. What might have happened would have taken images, community, and mastery and turned them into a complete, creative social studies/humanities unit. Such is the approach advocated by Jones and such are the relatively simple techniques used in this approach.

To further highlight this position and bring it closer to the reader, share in a recent experience of one of the authors while visiting relatives and friends in San Francisco. During his stay, he spent a lot of time with Ingrid, the wife of a graduate-school friend. At one point he had recommended some poetry by Paul Celan, in particular *Fugue of Death*. Late one Friday afternoon he was to pick up Ingrid at the public library. From there, they were to meet their spouses and all four were to go to dinner.

When the author arrived at the library, Ingrid was already waiting on the steps. She hurried to the car and a rush of words and feelings poured forth. She had spent the afternoon at the library preparing lessons for the upcoming school semester. Ingrid is an Eastern European protestant by birth, a language arts instructor at a junior college by profession. While working she remembered the poetry that had been strongly recommended. Finding a book in which several of Celan's poems were reproduced, she eagerly began *Fugue*. When she had finished it she was outraged. The poem had had such impact on her that she had let the book crash loudly to the floor. She had sat staring off into space for some time, overwhelmed by the vivid and horrifying images it conjured up and by the painful feelings it generated. She said that after what seemed an eternity she stormed over to the reading-room librarian and angrily protested the inclusion of the poem and the book in a public facility. The librarian stared back blankly and made some noncommittal remark about free speech. Ingrid indicated that the librarian must have thought her a fool or worse, "a lunatic."

In the car, she wondered aloud whether *Fugue* was poetry at all. Listening to her and gently feeding back both her feelings and her half-hidden thoughts, it became evident that much of her reaction was based not on the poem, but on an unconscious association to the poem. Ingrid had spent her early years wandering in war-torn Europe with all its terror and chaos. Several of her father's brothers became officers in the German Wehrmacht after the invasion of their homeland. The poem had stimulated memories and long-gone feelings of despair and helplessness. These insights were not long in coming into consciousness. And even with the relief that accompanied them Ingrid wondered whether any author had the right to "inflict" such affect and such imagery on an unsuspecting public. For Ingrid poetry was love and warmth, not darkness and evil.

Unfortunately, the librarian did not have the opportunity to see the evolution of the feelings and the resolution of the conflicts. When Ingrid returned both to apologize and to explain, the librarian could not remember the incident in question, perhaps not an uncommon event in a large library with many people wandering through it on any given day.

This example is dramatic, but does not overstate the need for sustained contact between librarian and patron. Perhaps some libraries are too large and too impersonal. If so, they could be restructured (as some schools have been restructured) to contain small libraries within the larger building. Obviously branches, storefront libraries, and bookmobiles are attempts to establish a sense of community. The need for the personnel who work in these establishments to open a dialogue with the people who come to them is one of the major points of this book.

Metaphoric Confluence

Jones provides the pedogogical rationale, instructional theory, and teaching skills to intertwine thoughts, feelings, and fantasies. The curious and poetic blends and harmonies of Samples's model, however, provide the framework for comprehensive confluence. Combining historicocultural speculation with contemporary brain research, Samples explores the rational and the metaphoric minds. What follows are the highlights and a summary of Samples's position. It would behoove the reader to go directly to the original source, *The Metaphoric Mind* (1976), for a fuller appreciation of the richness of this model.

What is the metaphoric mind? For Samples, it is the ghostlike, mystical mind; it is the mirror image of the rational mind. Containing no words, no structures, it is nature's own expression. It is found in myths and folklore as the interdependent relationship among all natural things, the interlocking puzzle that includes the bodies, minds, and souls of all living things.

The metaphoric mind is natural. It experiences time as cyclical and space as limitless; it views all things as unified. The rational mind, on the other hand, is cultural. It experiences linear time and limited space; it views all things as separate.

Samples argued persuasively that the metaphoric mind was in existence and in ascendancy preceding the advent and evolution of the rational mind. For Samples, the advent of language and symbols allowed the cultural to supplant the natural, the rational to supersede the metaphoric. Samples argued that language forced and still forces four discoveries on developing individuals, societies, and cultures, and these four conditions allow the ascent of the rational over the metaphoric. And yet even with these, the rational in no way completely overpowers the metaphoric. What are these four conditions?

First, the undifferentiated, holistic world as perceived cannot be communicated. It needs to be broken down and labeled. Thus, discrete words are attached to objects, experiences, events, and situations.

Where once there was a unified world, there now exist many separate entities. Second, these word-pieces of the newly fragmented world can be manipulated in different ways and organized in what is known as sentences. Third, the word-pieces cannot be put together randomly, but rather need to be strung together in certain grammatical ways. Fourth, this new separate world with its discrete word-pieces is not in fact magical; it is guided by logic. Indeed, Samples points out that throughout recorded history and at present the function of cultural institutions was and is to assist in gaining new words and new meanings, in refining language use, in helping people become more logical; all of this at the expense of the natural and the metaphoric.

These contrasting views of unity and separateness, of magical and logical, of cyclical and linear, of natural and cultural, of metaphoric and rational are not only conveniences, but are also real. Moreover, they reflect a separation of function and style in the cerebral hemispheres. For instance, from early times to the present, opposing beliefs have been held about right- and left-handedness. The right hand has always been associated with virtuousness, rationality, and stability; the left always with deviance, emotionality, and unreliability. Similarly, knowledge was believed to be acquired and used differently depending on handedness. "Right-handed knowing" was the province of priests, law-makers, and scientists. "Left-handed knowing" was the realm of artists, poets, and writers of prose and drama.

That these myths were only in part mythological has been demonstrated by recent research in cerebral hemisphere functioning. The left cerebral hemisphere (connected to and influencing the right side of the body) is responsible for sequential language and linear time sequences. It is the logical organizer that uses a convergent process moving toward a single, most logical outcome. The right cerebral hemisphere (connected to and influencing the left side of the body) is responsible for holistic perceptions and relationships. It is the creator that uses a divergent, expanding process moving toward new, previously unlinked patterns (Ornstein, 1972). Damage to the left hemisphere interferes with language, writing, analytic thinking, and ordering objects or symbols in sequence. Damage to the right hemisphere disrupts the ability to draw; to create music; the capacity to visualize spacial relationships or to perceive depth; and the skills to do visual or tactile maze-puzzles. Although the anatomical-morphological proof is scanty at present, it is not a wild inferential leap to argue that the cerebral hemispheres are the seats of the dual mind, given the separation of functioning that is so evident. Do not left-side functions reflect the rational mind? Likewise, do not right-side functions mirror the metaphoric mind? Ornstein in

time. Such a focus provides learners with a view of the various representations offered by a number of different people about how objects, processes, or conditions impacted and shaped both the person and sociocultural order.

Fifth, since the primary source of metaphor is nature, a core course in all educational settings would focus on the person-nature interface. Focusing on the delicate and ever changing relationship among living things, it would provide learners with opportunities to experience the infinitely repatternable elements of the natural order, to feel the cycles and metamorphoses, to view the limitlessness of space and time, and to understand the unity among all entities. This would be more than a typical ecology course. In addition to the ecosystem emphasis it would, through the various metaphoric modes, make connections for the learner in the best shamanistic tradition. Through symbolic metaphors, comparative metaphors, integrative metaphors, and inventive metaphors, it would touch on the vital interdependence of the natural order and undo the exclusive reliance on cultural linearities upon which most educational procedures are based. As Merlin did for the young Arthur and as Don Juan did for Castaneda, so would these natural metaphors and balanced experiences do for learners. It would help learners know how causes are effects, movers are moved by their motion, past is future, and how "Every star melts as surely as every snowflake . . . only to be born again in another time, another place" (from *Where All Things Belong*, an Essentia film, 1976).

From the authors' perspective, the library is the central place in which both confluence models might well be carried out. It is only in the library that all materials are readily available. Only the library provides readily available space. The library is the educational component with the variety and the flexibility necessary for exploration of the rational and the metaphoric. Consider the example of the tetrahedron.

That the library is a primary storehouse of knowledge, information, books, and words is evident. What is less evident is that it is also a primary storehouse of the various metaphoric modes. To be more specific, the *symbolic mode* exists whenever and wherever an abstract or visual sign is substituted for some object, some process, or some condition; for example, the alphabet, numerals, and logos. Consider the Dewey decimal system, dictionaries, reference books, and graphics displays. The *synergic-comparative mode* operates when two or more external objects, processes, or conditions are compared in such a way that both unite to become more than either one alone. Consider Noyes's famous line from *The Highwayman:* "The road was a ribbon of moonlight over the purple moor." Similarly, consider a copy of Chilton's repair manual for the Volkswagen "Beetle." The *integrative mode* occurs when physical-psychic attributes of a learner are extended into direct contact with objects, processes, and conditions outside of the self. Consider the overwhelming impact of Castaneda's quintet as it both describes and oftentimes facilitates the experiencing of this mode. Less dramatically and less spiritually, consider a beginning photographer's reactions as he sees his first enlarged print emerge from the developing bath in the darkroom of a media center. The *inventive mode* exists whenever a person creates a new level of awareness or of knowing as a result of self-initiated exploration of objects, processes, or conditions. Consider the "Ah-ha" experience of a student who finally comprehends Eliot's *The Waste Land* after rereading it with the aid of a critical essays book found in the library. Likewise, consider the now well-documented "high" generated by running experienced by the person who first became serious about running after reading Leonard's *The Ultimate Athlete* (New York: Viking, 1975) obtained from his local library or after seeing *The Loneliness of the Long Distance Runner* at the library's weekly film session.

Although experiences like those above can occur in other settings, it is the library and the library alone, with all its materials and media, that can and should provide the information and the atmosphere in which such experiences can occur repeatedly and in combination. The library need not be large and well equipped to provide the information and the atmosphere. Such an atmosphere can also occur in small, quiet, intimate libraries.

The reader is referred back to the sections of this chapter dealing with the linkages between the rational and the metaphoric and on the library as a storehouse of metaphoric modes. Review these sections. Expand on the examples given, and develop individualized ideas on how the library can strengthen its potential to engage the metaphoric as well as the rational mind. To get the reader started, the authors would like to offer several tentative suggestions:

1. Use the card catalog as an analogy stimulator. Use visuals and other symbols to cross-reference materials.
2. Replace word-signs with symbol-pictures to identify areas, parts of the collections, to present directions and instructions, to guide people in using library skills.
3. The library is not a fixed environment. Restructure it. Replace linear furnishings with more personal and more comfortable non-linear furnishings.
4. Designate certain areas as quiet, meditative places where people can go to think, contemplate, and fantasize.

5. In addition to film showings, have art displays and photography exhibits. In the same way, allow viewers to react to films, paintings or sculptures, and photographs in ways other than verbal discussion. For example, provide paint, charcoal, clay, and other media such as cameras for experimentation around the themes of any show, display, or exhibit.
6. Thematically group all materials in the collection. Do not isolate one medium from the others, nor one subject area from the others. Break the set that forces a librarian to contain all films in one area and all fiction in another, separate area. Likewise, integrate fact with fiction. The fiction of Heinrich Böll, for example, does as much if not more in capturing life in post–World War II Germany as the history or the films of that era.
7. "Green" the library. Hang a wide variety of plants all around the building.
8. Broaden the selection of speakers or lecturers. Include a variety of people who conduct experiential workshops on a multitude of topics. Sponsor talks and workshops for the general public.
9. Make better and wider use of the complex numbering schema available for all subject matter. See the title of chapter 8 in this book.
10. Design studios and laboratories for resident artists and scientists and for the general public. Have these specialists give lessons to the public.
11. Be creative. Take these suggestions, reject them, modify them, and develop an individualized, integrated, confluent library.

Some Commonalities

The two confluent models address the education of the complete person. They stress the inclusion of feelings, fantasies, and metaphors as well as thoughts as acceptable and important components of learning. Both deal with personality factors within the learner and within the facilitator. Both offer aids to current instructional methodology. They stress exercises and interactive procedures, questions and linking activities, and the alternating sequence of play and work as ways to tie content to process, to tie concepts to the learner, to tie thoughts to feelings and fantasies, and to tie the metaphoric to the rational. Such processes supplement current methods and enrich learning.

Both the models are clearly learner-centered. Although they stress to varying degrees materials and methods, they demand that content be made more personal and thus more relevant. When people are taken into account and worked with, when fantasies and feelings are made a real and legitimate part of learning, and when metaphor and play occur with regularity in the learning environment, the end result can only be more involvement, more commitment, more relevance, and more fun.

Closely related to the above are both models' motivational underpinnings. If learning is personalized and relevant, if it makes use of thinking, feeling, and fantasizing, and if it allows contact between the metaphoric and the rational, learning will be minimally anxiety-producing and minimally threatening. Both conditions are necessary for any learner's contact with the material and with the world around him. Both are required to insure breadth and depth in learning. Both are vital if the learner is to select and to learn based on an internal motive state that impels people toward effective transactions with their environment. By allowing maximal flexibility, familiarity, and contact, the models fit the newer, more complete view of motivation as competence-effectance. Learning is guided and directed by internal conditions rather than by external incentives or payoffs; learning is for impact and done with objects and with events that can be impacted, rather than for demands made by others or for any future good. In spite of their differences, then, the two models are closely related on several crucial core issues. Indeed they fit together well and provide the educator with a new perspective and a broad range of skills, approaches, and processes to enhance and enrich all forms of learning.

Strengths and Weaknesses

The chapter to this point clearly points out the strengths of the confluent models. The major weaknesses relate to the models' complexities and to the additional demands placed on educators.

Not without validity, the models point to the need for educators to develop a more than passing knowledge of personality, self-concept, or brain functioning, as well as a more complete understanding of teaching-learning methodologies, learning styles, motivation, and the nature and quality of learning. By making an already complex process even more complicated, confluence runs the risk of becoming convoluted and unmanageable. By dealing with a complicated process in a complex manner, confluence becomes a subject of confused and confusing criticism and the focus for angry jokes. Its complexities allow many educators to ignore it at a time when ignoring and ignorance are the last things teaching-learning needs.

Again, not without validity, both approaches demand change at a time when the social concern pendulum is swinging toward conservatism. They demand an experimental attitude and a flexibility that appear to go against the emerging cry for a return to the basics. They require more expenditures at a time when budgets are being scrutinized and cut drastically.

Because confluence views learning as a multifaceted process, considerable attention and effort have been spent developing lessons, strategies, and approaches for presenting content, personal, and social materials. Yet there is little evidence that correspondingly equal time or energy are going into the development of measurement-assessment tools. Confluent education ultimately will stand or fall on its ability to compare with the present, albeit inadequate, educational process. For confluent educators either to sit by patting themselves on the back for doing different things that "feel good" or to assume that traditional measures will tap the complex varieties of learning generated in confluent settings would be disastrous.

Along similar lines, the assumption that traditionally trained educators can conduct confluent learning experiences is faulty. The complexities of the learner, the teacher, the material, and the processes demand new sensitivities and skills. Apparently only a few teacher-training programs are designed to prepare truly confluent educators. This is particularly the case with library-science training programs. This is a sorry state of affairs since the library is the one complete, confluent learning center.

The Triple-Play Fantasy:
A Case Study

During the summer of 1977, one of the authors was staffing a workshop on humanistic education at a small New England college. Parenthetically, the workshop was attended by more than a proportionate number of public school librarians. For several days the group had been attempting to relate to one member who not only had come to the program with more than a modicum of skepticism and a clear expectation to learn nothing, but also had stated so publicly to all the participants. One evening he had offered that most if not all participants were "somewhat neurotic." At long last the situation crystallized when he asked permission to leave but with a contingency—that he receive the three credits attached to the course. This provocative request was met by anger, frustration, anxiety, and concern. The author, in conjunction with his cotrainer, refused to decide the issue one way or the other. The group was unwilling to involve itself. Instead, the man was asked to spend the morning writing an evaluation of the program, including his concerns and reasons both for desiring to leave and for obtaining credit for partial completion. He agreed. This position did much to heighten the above-mentioned feelings of discomfort and discontent.

Close to the end of the morning session, Ralph (a fictitious name intentionally used to protect the innocent, the guilty, or both) returned to share his evaluation. Expressing bad feelings toward the state Department of Education that had a policy requiring a certain number of re-certification credits for every five years of teaching and protesting his own psychological health, he assailed the program, the trainers, and the participants for their "absurdity," for their "lack of psychological well-being." He closed his presentation by stating that he "deserved" full credit because he received exactly what he expected from the workshop, nothing, and because he had received credit for a number of longer programs in which he had received as much and for a number of shorter programs in which he had received more. The co-trainers reasoned and explained that, since learning was more crucial than credits, since learning occurred only with willingness and with caring, and since Ralph, by his own acknowledgment, had reached his optimal level of learning, he could indeed leave with the knowledge that he would receive full credit. The participants, though noticeably uncomfortable, declined to persuade him otherwise.

That afternoon a decision was made to devote a portion of the time to discussing what had transpired. There seemed to be an inordinate amount of bad feelings still present. To begin, a body check, a technique designed to locate, focus, and highlight the psychosomatic nature of feelings, was conducted. During this check and during the subsequent lively discussion of feelings regarding the incident, the author was aware of a persistent, intrusive fantasy. At a propitious, although admittedly self-determined time, he shared it.

Sequentially, it went as follows. The author found himself in a rather peculiar and somewhat impoverished room. The other members of the group were present but, with the exception of Ralph, were ghostlike in form and blended with the pasty white walls. The author was working on Ralph, who was strapped to a laboratory table with a number of crude scientific and electrical instruments around him. Throughout the scene, the author repeatedly murmured, "I shall create it, I shall create it!" The scene suddenly shifted. Now the author found himself dressed as a knight-errant in a dying landscape. With a lance he was confronting a large windmill that bore a remarkable resemblance to Ralph. The windmill appeared to be intimidating the ghostlike representations of the other members. The author charged the windmill, with more than a modicum of reluctance, only to be knocked down again and again. Then, the scene suddenly shifted. The author and the group members

were sitting in a round room. They watched quietly and with looks of serenity as Ralph turned his back and walked out. All slowly nodded their heads one time. The fantasy at this point ended rather abruptly.

The author's interpretation, shared with the participants, dramatically came to mind. The author experienced himself first as a "Dr. Frankenstein" attempting to create interest, commitment, caring, and attempting to breathe life into a "dead Ralph." The ghosts represented the fear that, if this could not be done, the other group members would also "die" at the hands of their own feelings and fantasies. Second, the author experienced himself as Don Quixote trying "to dream the impossible dream . . . to reach the unreachable star . . . to beat the unbeatable foe" and hence to free the ghostlike group members from "the unrightable wrong" done them. Third, the author experienced himself and the group members accepting, though sadly, the loss of a member.

Resolution was reached after the interpretation with a marked lessening of tension and anxiety and with a noticeable increase in involvement (i.e., community), in experimentation, and in mastery. In retrospect, the author's fantasy and his interpretation served to represent the collective feelings, images, and thoughts of the group. The sharing of the fantasy and of the interpretation released all the participants from a painful and unnecessary burden, that of being responsible for Ralph and for his feelings, fantasies, thoughts, and behaviors.

AN EXERCISE

Confluent Problem Solving

Listed below are several theoretical situations in which a librarian must decide on a course of action. The authors have listed a variety of possible responses that involve cognitive, affective, and confluent behavior. Examine these in terms of your decision making in similar "critical incidents." Describe your behavior, your motives, your feelings, your attitudes and values, as well as your logic and intellectual responses concerned with such situations. How might the situation be handled better, worse, etc. ? Which of the listed choices would you have included in your responses ? Which include affective, cognitive, or confluent responses ? Which response is the least like your own ? Why ? Note: there are no wrong answers, although some would be considered incomplete in terms of confluence.

Situation 1—In defending a challenged policy do you:

1. State or reiterate the logical, documented facts and expect that policy will thereafter be followed without question?

2. Describe your beliefs concerning policy and the way you personally feel about following this particular policy, and expect or hope that a person will believe as you do and will cooperate or not as they feel best?

3. Describe the historical background, the logical development of the policy, then share your opinion of that policy and invite discussion based on feelings and rational appraisal of the strengths and weaknesses of the policy including suggestions for change?

Situation 2—In designing a change in an old policy or a new policy do you:

1. Study carefully the reasons for needed change, listing pros and cons, weighing carefully the consequences in terms of program success or failure?

2. Base conclusions and designs for action on careful study of documented evidence, surveys, etc., that you have collected?

3. Inform everyone involved that you have decided to institute a change, clearly describing the reasons why, and then ask for cooperation of all concerned?

4. Have an intuitive understanding that the policy is not working, that something is wrong somewhere?

5. Examine your own attitudes and feelings after talking with others about how they feel, what their attitudes are on present procedures, in order to determine how much they value them?

6. Inform everyone informally that you have made a decision to change policy based on what you feel to be most comfortable for them and for yourself?

7. During everyday interaction with other members of the library staff note their attitudes, feelings, and values concerning policy, share your feelings and ask for theirs concerning the present policy, and compare affective factors with rational, logical factors involved in the need for change?

8. Base conclusions and designs for action on careful study of documented facts as well as acknowledged feelings of all concerned, and involve all participating staff in designing the changes needed and in carrying out a policy that everyone finds most acceptable or least offensive?

Situation 3—In handling a complaint about the content of a book or other library media that has distressed a person do you:

1. Tell the person he has a right to his own opinion, but the library exists so that everyone can find what he wants? Tell him that he does not have to read anything that he does not want to?

2. Apologize, taking the blame for having allowed such a book to be part of the collection and make plans immediately to remove the book, if not forever, at least until this person moves away or dies?
3. Find the critical reviews that praise the book and engage the reader in an intellectual debate on the values of the book, author, theme, etc.?
4. Hand him a complaint form and withdraw quietly from the scene?
5. Sympathize with the reader, pat him on the back, and tell him that there are other less disturbing books that you can help him find?
6. Listen to the reader express his feelings about the book, allow him to criticize it if he wishes, and ask him if there is anything you can do to help? Follow through, if possible, including handing a complaint form if requested or finding another book more appropriate for the reader?

Practical Suggestions for
Incorporating Confluent Techniques

In working with a child, an adolescent, or an adult who has just expressed some distress or anxiety about something she has read, viewed, heard, or experienced as part of the library program, consider the following.

DO:

1. Encourage her to express her feelings, to share what she has just experienced in a book, film tape, or the library material or activity.
2. Listen fully. Be present and aware of what is being said and how it is being expressed.
3. Empathize. Try to feel what she feels. Express your understanding of her attitudes and values even if you do not agree with her position.
4. Ask her questions that are open-ended and that allow her to complete the thoughts and feelings she is describing.
5. Share your own fantasies and attitudes if you feel that that will help her.
6. Make connections between fantasy and the real world, between affective and cognitive aspects of the subject.
7. Offer additional materials, sources, or activities that might help her deal effectively with her fantasies, feelings, attitudes, or values.
8. Leave opportunity for her to refuse or to request other suggestions.

DON'T:

1. Cut a person off who is trying to describe her reactions to something she has read, seen, or heard that has distressed her.
2. Prepare responses to her in your head while she is still speaking to you.
3. Argue with her or think of this as simply a social conversation (unless it really is) in which you want or need to get in your own opinion.
4. Belittle her expression of feelings, fantasies, or values, no matter how trivial or foolish they seem to be.
5. Intellectualize. Allow her to fulfill her need to talk out her feelings. She may or may not wish to discuss the subject on another level later.
6. Force or plan activities or materials in which she may have no interest or by which she may become more disturbed.

References

Brown, George Isaac. *Human teaching of human learning.* New York: Viking, 1971.

Jones, Richard M. *Fantasy and feeling in education.* New York: New York University Press, 1968.

Koestler, Arthur. *The act of creation.* New York: Dell, 1966.

Krathwohl, David R., Bloom, Benjamin S., and Masia, Bertram B. *Taxonomy of educational objectives.* Handbook II, *Affective domain.* New York: McKay, 1964.

Kubie, Lawrence S. *Neurotic distortion of the creative process.* Lawrence: University of Kansas Press, 1958.

Laing, Ronald D. *The politics of experience.* New York: Ballantine, 1967.

Leonard, George B. *The ultimate athlete: Re-visioning sports, physical education and the body.* New York: Viking, 1975.

Ornstein, Robert E. *The nature of human consciousness: A book of readings.* San Francisco: W. H. Freeman, 1973.

———. *The psychology of consciousness.* New York: Penguin, 1972.

Samples, Bob. *The metaphoric mind.* Reading, Mass.: Addison-Wesley, 1976.

Silberer, Herbert. On symbol-formation. In David Rappaport (ed.), *Organization and pathology of thought.* New York: Columbia University Press, 1951.

5 The Value of Values Clarification

The Scene: A classroom in which the American Library Association's controversial film, *The Speaker*, has been shown. The government teacher begins discussion by asking the class to define the issue. Four students respond readily to the question, each seeing the question from a different perspective. The first answers that free speech is the issue. The second states that the students' right to decide what is to be presented in their school assemblies is at stake. The third is concerned with the rights of black students and others in the film who might be offended by the racist speakers. The fourth feels that the issue is the speaker's right to be protected from violence, whatever his opinions.

At first the discussion is soft-spoken and relatively emotion-free. An undertone develops, however, as the teacher probes to find out if students know what their own rights are as citizens of this country; if they know what the First Amendment means and what free speech sometimes involves. At one point a student says that the principal of the school in the film should not have prevented the speaker from presenting his views at the school, that he should not have stood in the way of the speaker's rights. The government teacher counters, "If you were the principal, then, you would allow the man to speak, even if you knew that some of your students would be deeply offended, and that a breach between those for and against the speaker might cause real anguish, possibly even violence?" The student responds, "Yes, because those students who are against the speaker's position don't have to go to the assembly if they do not wish to hear what he has to say. The man has a right to speak. They have the right not to listen." The government teacher then adds, "Even if you get many angry telephone calls, perhaps even threats from irate parents trying to pressure you not to allow the speaker?" Again the student replies, "Yes. That would make me all the more determined." The government teacher then says, "Even if your job is on the line and you have just been told that if you allow the speaker to come to the school your contract will not be renewed for the following year?" At this point the student pauses. It is obvious that she has developed empathy for the principal. She is on the spot and the teacher knows it. Then she disengages herself emotionally and says, "But that wouldn't really happen, would it?"

The teacher has done what he intended to do. Through a kind of Socratic dialogue he has brought the student to the edge of reality. She will have a better understanding when he is finished of how difficult it is to support really important values.

There are additional issues involved for those who see *The Speaker* because, unfortunately for ALA, the issue of free speech has boomeranged. It is ironical that ALA's Intellectual Freedom Committee, which set out with the best of intentions to reinforce the value of free speech and its associated freedoms, the rights to read and to write, ran headlong into some of ALA's own members who felt that the content of the film was so objectionable, so harmful, that they wanted to prevent it from being shown, at least under ALA's sponsorship. If the film actually helps perpetuate racist attitudes, even support them, as a number of people believe, then the Intellectual Freedom Committee is faced with a paradox; the conflict between their wish to film what they believe is a valid message about freedom of speech and ALA's commitment to its membership to support the other important values of equality and justice for all people.

Value conflicts are not uncommon in areas that concern such things as religion and politics. Other areas rich in value problems are race, family, sex, male-female roles, poverty, energy, health, money, personal habits, and so forth. Values clarification specialists believe that people should possess a set of valuing skills, a process for clarifying and developing values that will stand them in good stead when conflict or confusion does arise (Kirschenbaum, 1976). In values clarification, no "official value(s)" are set up as goals. Rather the recognition of the importance of valuing is emphasized as part of the ongoing development of human behavior. A person's life, as well as the particular choices she makes, will have positive meaning and will also be constructive socially. While no guarantees are offered that this will occur if values clarification is incorporated into one's life, the likelihood increases as the use of the skills becomes a part of daily living (Kirschenbaum, 1977).

The use of these techniques is not limited to personal valuing. They may be incorporated in any learning or working situation as the need to examine one's own values or the values of others arises. Over twenty studies (Kirschenbaum, 1976) have been conducted that center on the use of values clarification with teachers, grade school children, high school students, student teachers, juvenile delinquents with drug problems, and pregnant minor women. The rationale behind the inclusion of values clarification in learning and working situations is that students and others not only can make decisions about their values, but that they have a need and a right to do so. As discussed in chapter 1, the educational climate of the 1960s brought about a change in the class-room. Students were recognized as human beings who could serve as more than simple repositories for their teachers' knowledge and skills, and education was seen to be more than just brain training or the mastery of cognitive skills. To help a student understand what it is that she values, what she is willing to choose to act upon, became a part of education too.

The first significant milestone in values clarification was a book called *Values and Teaching*. Published in 1966, it was the joint effort of three innovative students of values: Louis Raths, Merrill Harmin, and Sidney B. Simon. Louis Raths was the originator of the concept of values clarification. Workers in the field can be grateful that he did not jealously guard his methods or copyright his techniques, but, rather, generously shared them with students and colleagues alike. Raths put into practice what was described above—the emancipation of students as choicemakers. By asking students more questions he was forcing them to decide what was important to learn or to act upon and thus to exer-cise their value system, to test it out. In the introduction to *Values and Teaching*, Kimball Wiles, one of Raths's former students, explains his first reaction to the difference between Raths's approach and that of all the other teachers he had known. "As far as I could detect he never really approved any statement I made. He would ask a question, make a noncommittal observation, test my assertion by supplying addi-tional data, ask if I had considered a different alternative" (Raths, Harmin, and Simon, 1966, p. vii).

If this sounds more like a librarian helping a person find and evaluate material on a subject than a teacher working with a student, most people can understand why Wiles found this approach remarkable. Like many students he expected the teacher to be more directive, provide answers, and reinforce rather than offer more questions. This kind of response to a student has now become fairly well accepted as a teaching strategy, one used successfully by a significant number of educators and some other individuals in the "helping" professions. Raths, however, was the first person to bring together a scholarly rationale behind the technique and to preach what he practiced successfully. The work was directed at what he felt was a major concern: people's "clarity of relationship to society" (Raths et al., p. 4). At one end of a continuum he considered people to be "positive, purposeful, enthusiastic and proud," but at the other he listed those who were "apathetic, flighty, very uncertain, very inconsistent, drifters, overconformers, overdissenters, and poseurs or role players" (Raths et al., pp. 5–6). These people are unable to formulate a set of consistent values that will balance involvement with freedom.

Raths offered credit to John Dewey for having a significant impact on his work, but for Raths there was a shift of emphasis from Dewey's concern for the *content* of values and the need for specific identifiable values to the need for a *process* of valuing. The valuing process is a means to an end, which is to help people see what it is they want most in their lives so that they can pursue their goals with integrity and joy.

The Process

How to help a person clarify and establish her values without stepping on her self image is the basis of techniques developed in *Values and Teaching*. The approach involves concerned listening, a certain type of questioning that arises out of careful attention, and a responsive reflective answering that paraphrases the speaker's concern rather than that of the listener. Moralizing and lecturing are considered out of place in this kind of dialogue. Instead the object is to help the person determine for herself if what she values is, in fact, desirable.

The seven steps in which a person may become involved when making a value decision are: (1) choosing freely; (2) choosing from among alternatives; (3) choosing after thoughtful consideration of the consequences of each alternative; (4) prizing and cherishing; (5) publicly affirming; (6) acting upon choices; and (7) repeating, or acting with a pattern or consistency (Raths et al.). By asking questions or paraphrasing the speaker, the facilitator helps the individual to help herself.

Some assumptions are naturally made by Raths and his colleagues in all of this. The first is that people value "valuing," an assumption that is not too difficult for most people to accept. The second and more controversial assumption is that people should help others with their thinking about values. Values clarification is thought to promote the values of thinking, feeling, choosing, communicating, and acting. Critical thinking is regarded as better than noncritical thinking; considering consequences is regarded as better than random or thoughtless choosing; free choice is considered better than simply yielding to authority or peer pressure (Kirschenbaum, 1971). All of these are ends toward which the advocates of values clarification work. Thus, they respond to the criticism that their work is "value free," "hedonistic," and "superficial." One values clarification author states that, "If we support moral reasoning, then we value justice. If we advocate divergent thinking, then we value creativity. If we uphold free choice, then we value autonomy or freedom. If we encourage 'no-lose' conflict resolution, then we value equality" (Kirschenbaum, 1976, p. 104). To the charge that values clarification is considered "relativistic" they reply with less certainty, saying that some people who use values clarification believe that there are absolute values and others do not, and that proof of the value of such a thing as "justice" is not possible through research (Kirschenbaum, 1976).

Alternatives

Other people's values do, then, apparently affect what an individual does and how she behaves; and in turn the individual also affects those in her sphere of influence. If, in fact, a person chooses to care about what happens to others, there are several possible courses of action in addition to values clarification. As Howard Kirschenbaum suggests, people may moralize, may model their own values (i.e., show by their choices what they truly value); they may simply despair, or they may take a laissez-faire attitude. But for those who are interested in values clarification, modeling one's own values is only second best as a sign of caring for others and the alternatives are poor substitutes. Persuading through argument, limiting someone's choices, establishing rules and regulations, using rewards and punishments, appealing to guilt or to one's conscience, using dogma or other unquestioned wisdom are also considered less beneficial and less lasting. Compared to a process in which a person helps develop values that can be used for a lifetime (by someone with whom the person may or may not be in close contact), such methods have less staying power, less carry-over (Kirschenbaum, 1977).

Librarians and Values Clarification

During the summer of 1977 the authors visited one of the largest public libraries in the state of Maine. They ventured off a beautiful island to find materials that would help in the writing of this chapter, especially materials on the historical background of values clarification. They checked the card catalog and found not one of the principal books on the subject. Reflecting later on the lack of those titles reminded them that values clarification is relatively young as a model and its use has been limited to the fields of education, psychology, and social work, for the most part. The public library visited in 1977 is very close to the largest branch of the state university, where many books related to these fields are undoubtedly housed. Still, the fact that there were no books readily available for the general public reinforced their belief that a need existed for more information on the subject for librarians.

The authors were reminded, too, of the previous spring when they had attended a regional New England conference of school librarians and media specialists at which their programs were the only humanistic education offering on a wide bill of fare. It was also the first workshop on values and group dynamics ever to be presented to that group. The authors' objectives were to introduce a particular consensus method for working in groups. In order to do that they chose a rather interesting exercise that asks that people work together until they can agree on the rank ordering of twenty values held by young people. There was a specific order to the twenty; it was to be revealed at the end during a wind-up discussion. The librarians were asked to prioritize the list as they thought young people would, not as they themselves would personally. Each person was asked to do the list alone initially, then each group would work together until they reached consensus or their allotted time was up. They were asked to share their experience with and knowledge of young people in doing this task, and were asked not to use a majority-voting format. They were also asked not to "horse-trade" or hold out until they won a point. They were to work towards a list that they could accept comfortably as a group.

After the groups had finished, resulting statistics were posted to show how each group came out in relation to the others and to the established rankings. The concept of "synergy" was discussed, along with the benefits of working as a group rather than as individuals. The authors also delved into how people felt about the exercise as well as about its content.

The authors found very few librarians who did not see some value in knowing how the values of young people were prioritized. A few, however, found it inappropriate to have the values presented in the particular format used. They felt that there was no value to prioritizing because they felt sure young people would never come to agreement about those twenty values themselves. In other words, they were unwilling to accept the findings.

To the authors, the most interesting reaction came from those librarians who simply could not detach themselves from their own value system long enough to do the exercise. The priorities they used during the workshop were their own and they engaged in heated argument over the exact value, the exact ranking of each item on the list. When on occasion these librarians were reminded by a member of their own group that they were supposed to be dealing with young peoples' values, the authors observed perplexed expressions that seemed to register how very difficult it was for them to make the distinction. Almost as if there had to be only one value system! Some librarians became defensive when reminded by their peers that they were using their own values. Others worked hard to avoid mixing up their own values with what they believed young persons would value.

It was not an easy exercise—reaching consensus never is. Reaching consensus about values is probably one of the more difficult group endeavors. If for no other reason, the authors concluded that the workshops were of some help. They hope that these particular librarians will be increasingly conscious of the importance of "valuing" in their work with people of all ages.

The practicing librarian is well aware of how widely diversified and complicated are the many value messages the world imparts to everyone. Sorting, selecting, classifying, cataloging the media and its messages in some sensible way are all tasks in this profession. Particularly when librarians engage in selection and evaluation of media, they are using techniques similar to those used in values clarification. Librarians should provide the most accurate, most complete information available whatever the subject's worth may be to them personally. It has never been their role to "sell" or editorialize one position or another.

Having established a relatively neutral posture when providing information, the librarian is not unlike the person who helps individuals reach their own conclusions in values clarification exercises. So, in a very real sense, librarians are particularly suited to take advantage of what the values clarification model has to offer this profession.

Values Clarification Techniques

The school librarian may have already discovered values clarification. Watching teachers involved in practicing this method, she may have seen that there is no real problem in transferring such approaches from the classroom to the media center or library. Although group work is part of values clarification it can also be used on a one-to-one basis. A teacher may, for instance, employ what is called a clarifying response to something a student says. The teacher will watch to see if the student recognizes for herself the value of an activity, attitude, behavior, or feeling.

Raths and his colleagues suggested that the teacher should ask, in a nonjudgmental way, questions that relate to one or more of the seven steps listed earlier in the chapter. For example, "Did you have to choose that—was it a free choice?" "Was that something you yourself selected or chose?" "Would you really do that or are you just talking?" "How far are you willing to go?" "Would you do the same thing over again?" "Do you do this often?" "Should you get other people interested and involved?" "Are you glad you feel that way?" According to their research, there are certain indicators that point toward possible development of a value; these are attitudes, aspirations, purposes, interests, and activities. Key words, for instance, that indicate attitudes and that are looked for by a facilitator are: "I'm for . . . ," "I'm against . . . ," "I feel that . . . ," "If you ask me . . . ," "My way is . . . ," "I'm convinced . . . ." Value indicators for aspirations show in statements that begin: "In the future . . . ," "Someday . . . ," "If all goes well . . . ," "When I grow up . . . ," and so on. A teacher comfortable with and skilled in values clarification techniques becomes comfortable in responding to such statements with variations on questions like the ones already described, or with paraphrases of what the student has just said in a matter-of-fact way. Sarcastic responses, put-downs, or objective lectures have no place in this technique. The government teacher described in the opening scene illustrated this approach by using questions that in effect asked, "How far are you willing to go?" and "Would you really do that or are you just talking?"

More complicated exercises are offered by values clarification exponents for incorporation into the usual activities that take place in schools. Ideally such exercises should be integrated into the subject matter daily, into ordinary dialogues between and among students and their teacher. Taught as a separate unit, values clarification can also be helpful. It may not, however, be seen as clearly related to the student's own life or not be reinforced often enough to have a degree of carryover into the student's day-to-day living, where she may need it most.

For the librarian interested in finding out about values clarification, a first step might be to attend a workshop. A participant in such a workshop may have done some reading beforehand, but more likely she has received firsthand information from a colleague or a friend who has participated in a values clarification program. At a typical workshop, the facilitator may begin by asking participants to make a list of those characteristics about themselves that they value most, and perhaps list one thing they value least and would like to change. Extensions of those characteristics might also be requested, such as those activities or possessions a person most enjoys. For a few newcomers this activity may stimulate uneasy feelings, perhaps even a sense of violation of privacy; they may even have difficulty finding anything to write down. Once begun, however, people generally become fascinated with their own lists and with the lists of others when they exchange lists at certain points in the session. The leader's approach is always gentle and nondemanding. There is a rule introduced at the very beginning of all values clarification workshops that says that the individual is free to bypass any activity that may cause her personal discomfort. People are never forced to do anything they do not wish to do.

A common way to begin sharing what people have written down is to ask participants to mill silently around the room after pinning their lists to their fronts. They are asked to make eye contact with others at some point while reading each others' lists, but not to speak or comment on others' values. This is perhaps the most difficult part. People frequently feel awkward with the silence. Usually there are occasional murmurs of approval, recognition of a shared interest through vigorous nodding of heads, through pats on the shoulder, and through laughter accompanying the proceedings.

Another type of exercise that usually follows in such a workshop is one in which people are asked to break up into small groups of two, three, or four. They are then asked to pick one or two characteristics of their own to discuss and to explain to their partner(s). Or they may be given a choice of several controversial subjects to discuss in terms of their own values. Each person will be given several minutes to speak. Each partner will be instructed to repeat carefully what she has heard. Then the first person will confirm whether that was, in fact, what was said. The procedure is then reversed, giving the listener opportunity to describe her own characteristics or opinions. The object is to give practice in articulating one's values, and to develop good listening, attending, and responding habits. Participants are asked to give full attention to the other person, to maintain eye contact as much as is comfortable, to abstain from critical comments or even from constructive suggestions. For many people this may be the beginning of a whole new way of interacting with others. If they are accustomed to formulating their own responses while giving only partial attention to a speaker, they may not hear everything being said. What values clarification seeks is the development of basic skills that are seldom if ever taught in traditional schools or at home: listening, attending, and responding empathically.

A third type of exercise has to do with empathic feedback. Again exercises will be conducted in dyads or in small groups. Each person may be asked to describe something she has done or some opinion she holds that has been particularly difficult for her. The listener(s), regardless of her own value viewpoint that may or may not be opposed to the other person's, must, at the end of the description, find some way of expressing understanding of the other person's viewpoint or action. She will not be asked to condone, but rather to empathize, to put herself in the other person's position, and to state her recognition and appreciation of what the other person experiences. A variation of this exercise asks each individual to find some positive attribute of her partner and to express this using eye-to-eye contact, sometimes holding the other person's hands.

Uncovering or rediscovering and sharing one's values can be a delightful experience. When workshops are directed by trained personnel few people go away from such exercises feeling distressed in any way. There is evidence, instead, that positive carry-over extends for some time into everyday life (Kirschenbaum, 1976). The impact of sharing good feelings encourages people to articulate and reaffirm their positive values and beliefs more often.

Strengths and Possible Uses

"The life which is unexamined is not worth living" (Socrates, *The Apology*, 470–399 B.C.). Although the research results mentioned above are not yet entirely conclusive, at least twenty-two studies have already been completed. Nineteen of those are described and summarized individually in an article by Howard Kirschenbaum (1976). Although Kirschenbaum does not attempt to reach conclusions collectively, it is fairly evident that, except for one, all of the studies show positive correlation between valuing and personal growth and achievement. In addition Kirschenbaum states that therapy done by Rogers and Dymond in 1954 indicated that "as clients gain greater awareness of their own inner experience, including what they truly prize and cherish, their self-esteem increases and they are less likely to repeat the destructive behavior that might have brought them into therapy" (Kirschenbaum, 1976, p. 113).

Of particular interest to librarians (who may be concerned with the "back-to-basics" hew and cry) is a study conducted by Eleanor Pracejus (1975) that compared gains in reading comprehension between one group of eighth graders who had twelve sessions of story discussion using a values clarification approach and one group that read the same stories and followed the publisher's suggested discussion approach. The values clarification group had significantly greater reading comprehension.

The primary strengths of values clarification lie in its ability to help people become aware of what their real concerns and values are and to understand them in a social context as they relate to others' values. Values clarification helps a person to set her priorities and to accept responsibility for her choices by developing a concern for the consequences of her position. It helps develop communication skills in listening, attending, responding, and providing feedback.

Positive Personal Support

Aside from documented strengths, the authors' own personal perspective indicates that values clarification builds good feelings and creates a kind of natural "high" that helps individuals see and accept the positive aspects of themselves and others. Although people may all feel that they are capable of seeing and accepting positive attributes in others, society teaches most to minimize their own good characteristics and attributes. Values clarification works toward undoing the kind of response that dismisses someone's kind words. Anyone turning aside a compliment with a "humble pie," self-negating reaction, answering, "Oh, it's nothing, really," is exhibiting this kind of social pattern. Values clarification teaches that it is all right to center positively on oneself, to understand one's own personal needs, and to appreciate and accentuate good qualities. It teaches ways to incorporate that understanding and appreciation into learning situations as well as into everyday living. In addition, it encourages positive support for others so that they too can share in the wealth of good feelings.

Faults and Abuses

The alleged weaknesses described earlier in the chapter (i.e., the criticisms holding that values clarification has no values itself, that it is hedonistic and superficial as well as relativistic) are answered sufficiently for these purposes by values clarification practitioners quoted earlier in the chapter. Other faults and abuses of values clarification should also be noted, however.

At times values clarification can be like a "closed club" or a social organization. It can develop the exclusive characteristics of the sorority or the fraternity. Novices witnessing some of the interactions among the initiated may feel put off, even unreceptive to trying out any of the activities offered at workshops. Having heard reports second- or third-hand, without even attending a meeting, many people make up their minds that there is something unsavory and suspicious about all that rejoicing and good feeling. There may be misperceived sexual overtones that in some cases emanate from so-called skin hunger sessions that frighten some people and encourage others for the wrong reasons. In actuality, "skin hunger" sessions focus on learning to touch for comfort and for affection, to give the nonsexual nurturing that is a widely acknowledged need of all human beings. Yet these sessions are inevitably misinterpreted by some individuals, giving values clarification sessions a less than pristine reputation.

A variation on the problem may follow when an initiate goes home, having been convinced of the genuineness of the values clarification climate, and tries to introduce some of the exercises to her family or her colleagues. She may be greeted with derision or disbelief. She may feel like giving someone a hug and become suddenly aware that it simply will not work out as she intended. Some people do not like to be touched and their wishes must be respected, as disappointing as it may be to the person who wishes to touch.

Another criticism is that the carry-over may not last very long from even the most intensive and successful of workshops. Upon returning to an environment that may be relatively nonsupportive, the person who has felt really delighted with values clarification experiences may quickly revert to old methods of dealing with people around her, rather than court rejection on all sides.

The reverse of this situation, however, can also create shortcomings. Occasionally a person will become hooked on values clarification. A "true believer," she will spend all her time and energy with the system to the exclusion of other concerns. She may have picked up only one or two points that she feels are special, but she will practice these points to the exclusion of everything else. She may, for instance, center so much on herself that it becomes difficult for others to communicate with her. Obviously this is precisely the opposite of the intent of values clarification, but it does happen.

Accompanying this is the allegation that values clarification is anti-intellectual. Whether or not that assertion is valid depends entirely upon individual practitioners, since the method is subject to the intellectual behavior and aptitudes of its practitioners. Some teachers, for instance, easily combine cognitive content and skills with values clarification methods, just as the government teacher was doing at the beginning of the chapter. Others may use the model as a welcome means of escape from the curriculum. This can be good or bad. One of the strengths of the model, its very flexibility, also becomes one of its weaknesses when it is abused by unpracticed, untrained enthusiasts.

Values clarification is, therefore, vulnerable to attack by people who demand an unyielding discipline and a clear-cut, right-or-wrong, black-or-white format. At the same time there is a formulistic nature to values clarification, the kind of recipelike approach to exercises that may lead to boredom after initial exposure to the model. If the use of exercises becomes routine, the process may lose its impact and effectiveness. Like all models, values clarification needs contrast and should be integrated into whatever else is going on in the environment, wherever it is practiced.

Values clarification is subject to cultism and, as mentioned before, this can lead to the "true-believer" syndrome. It can also lead to a "power trip" for some of the leaders that may have detrimental effects both on participants and on the model. When the first euphoric experience is underway at a successful workshop, some participants may become overly optimistic and expect too much in the way of "personal salvation" from whatever personal problems they may have brought with them. Extreme gratitude to the leader(s) sometimes results when a person who has never been listened to and who has lacked affection suddenly feels recognized and cared for for the first time in her life. This is a ticklish situation, even for the best leaders; but for those who are overly impressed with their own power it may become dangerous. The authors have personally witnessed the paradox of leaders who bend over backwards to be "equal" and thereby set themselves apart from the group. They have seen the "guru" enjoy the worship of selected members of groups: therein lies one of the greatest abuses of the model. Fortunately it is not widespread. Successful facilitators are usually trained through apprenticeships with people who have studied with or who are members of the National Humanistic Education Center. Howard Kirschenbaum, one of the more recent leaders of the movement, has expressed his concern for the inexperienced facilitator in *Advanced Value Clarification* (Kirschenbaum, 1977). This book is designed to help just such people, but anyone interested in values clarification will most certainly benefit if she studies the book carefully and follows the directions offered there.

A Model for Librarians

From the authors' point of view, values clarification is general enough and valuable enough as a model to be adopted for use anywhere by anyone who wishes to put it to work. Any time people wish to center on the values involved in a particular occurrence or interaction, it can be used to facilitate communication, to help people become more responsive and empathic to the needs of others. For librarians it has particular worth in situations such as the following:

1. The interpersonal contacts each librarian has on the job. Librarians are quite likely to encounter the expression of many personal concerns, requests for information on highly delicate subjects. Librarians are not generally considered threatening to talk to. Unlike teachers, for instance, librarians do not usually become involved in grading or testing individuals on a regular basis. They are also less likely to have the kinds of discipline problems that occur in the classroom. If students and adults who use libraries have frequent contact with a nonthreatening person who helps them find information and who discusses a variety of topics in an open and friendly fashion, a relationship may develop that allows people to say what they are feeling on any number of subjects. This may not always be to the librarian's personal preference. She may be too busy to stop and respond to the person with a crucial need to talk; she may not want to get involved. Sometimes a person obviously needs specialized counseling and the librarian feels unequipped to handle what appears to be a serious problem. More often than not, however, these situations are not typical. In the ordinary course of events conversation evolves in a normal way and there are endless opportunities to help people clarify what they feel about their choices, their actions, or their plans. In using values clarification the librarian can choose to invest a little extra effort into what might otherwise have become routinized communication.

2. Reference work can be ticklish business. When reference questions are hazy or ill-defined, they may be masking the real information needs of a person. It is necessary for the skilled reference librarian to know how to approach, how to put herself in the questioner's place, in order to decode the real question or "the message behind the message." Empathic listening, attending, and responding are sometimes the only way to determine what is really on the questioner's mind.

3. When people work together as a team, there are lows and highs

in performance, lows and highs in morale. There comes a time when positive feedback and encouragement can play an important role in lifting spirits and renewing dedication. Administrators need to know when praise is needed, when recognition can make a difference in performance. For instance, it is vital for a worker to know what it is she does that is most valued, as well as those things she may do that are least valued and that need to be changed. Self-evaluation can include the opportunity for a person to write about or to speak to these issues, and then to hear from a supervisor or administrator who has the job of going over evaluation forms. In addition, members of a group need to know how to give each other support. Leaders, too, need to know when they are valued most and valued least. Later in the book disclosure and confrontation techniques will be discussed, techniques that help one to deal with the more unpleasant realities that may need discussion.

4. Whether there is a regularly appointed time for review and evaluation of the philosophy and goals of the library or whether individual citizens or staff take it upon themselves to comment upon or criticize library philosophy, values clarification can be helpful. Hearing what it is about the library that is troublesome to someone's value system may be very painful. Most often librarians think about the attacks of censors and shudder; however, a truly empathic response to a censor, a "soft answer" that shows an understanding of the value of this point of view, may indeed turn away wrath. In fact, the authors suggest that it is next to impossible to compose a "soft answer" that does not contain a little empathy for the antagonist personally, if not sympathy for her point of view.

5. When persons using the library lack a sense of responsible behavior in relation to library rules, regulations, and so forth, rather than using threats a "soft answer," a recognition of the good qualities of the person who is "misbehaving," may be called into play. Most people, for instance, will respond positively to notices of overdue books if reminded that the librarian knows that they would certainly want to share the books with others and that others will appreciate their consideration when they return the books promptly. Perhaps it takes more time and energy to approach a recalcitrant individual positively than negatively, but the results can be gratifying from a practical point of view. A librarian who does not use a fine system but instead uses posters that stress and value the responsibility of borrowers who return

their books on time may have fewer book losses annually than the one who installs a warning system. The authors know of a case where annual inventory losses have gone down over the past three years and where borrowed books, as well as stolen ones, are returned in much greater numbers than they were in the years preceding this marked change in approach to readers.

Values clarification is not a panacea. It will not work all of the time in any situation. It takes time to learn to incorporate it into the daily procedures and conversations of the working routine. Remember that to use it the individual will need to develop an increased awareness of the other person, an ear attuned to values messages. If values clarification fails the first time, do not abandon it immediately. Only practice and determination will make it readily available to use skillfully and wisely, but such is the case with any skill worth having.

AN EXERCISE

A Personal Exploration

In writing this book the authors were reminded by the editors to scrutinize their readers closely. Could they justify their claim that the knowledge and skills offered have any value to librarians? Why librarians and not some other group? Who are librarians anyway that they should be interested in affective education and humanistic models of communication?

At this point, having discussed values clarification, the authors would like to turn the question over to the reader. Answer the following questions in writing, by taping, or by speaking directly to another person who will listen without comment until you have finished the entire exercise. Then, if you are working with another person, ask her to answer the questions while you listen.

Who are you? List the characteristics you value most about yourself as an individual. As a member of your profession. What are your goals in life? Which of your goals match comfortably the goals of the people with whom you work? Which of your professional values most nearly match a cherished personal value? Which professional value conflicts most with a personal value? Is your life what you want it to be? How well do you empathize with others? How well do you listen to others? How well do others listen to you? How do you check your perceptions of others? How do they check your perceptions of them? Who is your most valued colleague? Why? Who is the person who most threatens you on the job? Why? Which of your attitudes have changed in the last year? Which of your values? What things have changed about you since five years ago? Since yesterday? List the things about yourself that you value least professionally. As a human being. What are your plans for tomorrow? For five years from now?

Most people do not take the time to examine their lives periodically in this fashion. They assume they know the answers already. Surprisingly, when these same people engage in an exercise like the one above, they find that the results are gratifying. Whether one unconsciously knows the answers or not, articulating personal feelings about one's self is important.

Obviously there are no right or wrong answers in this exercise. There are only answers that fit an individual's situation. Having used this exercise in two workshops with a wide variety of librarians, the authors were fascinated to hear the many possible ways the list could be arranged and the reasons behind the arrangements. The emotional exchanges that resulted from sharing individual priorities more than proved the affective connection to the criteria. After you have tried this yourself, you might want to share it with colleagues and see what happens.

As you continue to read this book, keep in mind that everything said here can be, like the cloth from a fabric mill, tailored for personal use. It can be fashioned for you or passed on and shared with others. Anything here is available for enlargement, correction, amendment. You can ignore, argue with, enjoy, hate, or discount anything. It is your choice and clearly your right, if not your obligation, to do with it what you will. The authors hope only that you will hear them and then listen well—to yourself.

AN EXERCISE

Individual Affective Selection
Criteria

This exercise is not unlike some of those designed for students and teachers for values clarification. The difference is that here clarification of values is connected with the cognitive process of media selection. In becoming aware of your affective reasons for making choices and the affective reasons of others, you may be better equipped to defend your library's selection policy, a policy ideally designed to insure inclusion of all points of view in politics, religion, matters concerning sex, and other areas where controversy may arise.

Instructions: This exercise will require two blank sheets of paper, approximately 9 by 12 inches in size. Tear one sheet into twelve equal parts, and on the second sheet draw corresponding lines that divide the paper into twelve equal parts, matching the size of the small pieces of paper. The second piece of paper will be the game board, and the twelve small pieces will be arranged and rearranged on the board as you play. Number the squares on the game board from one to twelve and from left to right across the paper.

To begin the exercise, refer to the first two books described on the list below. Write them down (in abbreviated form) on two of the small pieces of paper. Now place one of the books on number one of your game board and the other on number two, according to your priorities. You must assume at this point that they are your only two choices and that one is more important than the other. After you have arranged them, refer to numbers three and four on the list. Write these two down on pieces of paper and, considering their importance in relation not only to each other but the other two already on the board, arrange all four pieces so that your first priority is in the number one place, number two in its place, and so on through number four.

During the course of play you will consider two choices at a time in relationship to what has already been placed on the board until you have completed the exercise. You will be rearranging the small pieces of paper frequently. The final outcome should show that your last six choices are those that you would not mind delaying or rejecting entirely. Although the game can be played simply by writing out all of the titles as you would arrange them according to final priority, it is not nearly as intriguing that way. For best results, the exercise should be done with at least two people.

The following books are those that you are asked to consider and renumber according to your own criteria. When you have completed your list, it should be evident that your choices were not exclusively objective.

( ) 1. A book on sexism in the public schools and what to do about it.

( ) 2. A book proselytizing a specific religious sect (offered by an evangelical citizen of the local community).

( ) 3. A book from the Best Books for Children or Young Adults by ALA.

( ) 4. A book on sex education presenting the case *against* sex before marriage.

( ) 5. A book on sex education presenting the case *for* sex before marriage.

( ) 6. A book recommended by a board member that she will use only once and that is very expensive.

( ) 7. A book recommended by a community leader who never uses the books she recommends.

(   ) 8. The top paperback in the country recommended by at least five students, but considered violent and in poor taste by some powerful adults in the community.

(   ) 9. A book of verse by the regional poetry club.

(   ) 10. A book of limited appeal requested by a person who has a special project. She seldom uses the library, but when she does she is most appreciative.

(   ) 11. A book recommended by the D.A.R. on the proper use of the flag.

(   ) 12. An art book being pushed by your favorite salesperson that she claims is being read all over the country.

After you have ranked your choices, put an *R* after those that would constitute the most risk in terms of citizen or board member objections. Put an *S* next to those that would be the safest choices and would offend the fewest people. How many *R*s were included in your first six choices? How many *S*s? How many of those marked *S* would you consider to be of less value to the collection as a whole and to your library users? How many of the *R*s? Do you feel certain about your choices in terms of all of your evaluative criteria and your selection policy? Do you feel annoyed with any of your choices? Compromised? Comfortable? If any feelings like those suggested above have crept into your consciousness, you may see that book and media selection does involve values. It is simply not a cut-and-dried affair, nor a totally objective one.

References

Kirschenbaum, Howard. *Advanced value clarification.* LaJolla, Calif.: University Associates, 1977.

———. Clarifying values clarification: Some theoretical issues and a review of research. *Group and organization studies,* 1976, *1*, 99–116.

Pracejus, Eleanor. *The effect of values clarification on reading comprehension.* Unpublished doctoral dissertation, University of Pittsburgh, 1975.

Raths, Louis E., Harmin, Merrill, and Simon, Sidney B. *Values and teaching.* Columbus, Ohio: Charles E. Merrill, 1966.

6 Love Thy Neighbor as Thyself

The Self-Awareness/Self-Esteem Paradox

The Scene: William sits in his study quietly sipping a scotch before beginning preparations for his dinner alone. The family is out for the evening. He likes the mindless chatter of talk shows because he can tune in or out as he unwinds from his usual hectic day, and so the television plays quietly in one corner of the room.

William is director of one of America's large public library systems. With a strong background in business, he feels that the economic state of the library is his biggest responsibility and challenge. He enjoys wheeling and dealing in finance. He does so with the highly competitive fervor of an athlete pitting himself against other players. The adequate funding of his library results directly from what he likes to think of as his aggressive tactics. William has brought new life and energy to a once failing institution and the city is obviously grateful as more and more people turn to the library for its services.

As William sits relaxing, he muses about two of the problems that have been bothersome over the past six months or more. If only Jonathan Thronly would stop playing games with the trustees and admit that this should be his last year as chairman of the board. After all, the old codger turned seventy-five this July, and even if he is in damn good health, anyone should know enough is enough. Perhaps he would have to force the issue. And if Rose Ann Heward would only shake up the personnel in Reference Services. Their performance dropped to an alarmingly low level when Alan Loft moved in as assistant director of that department. Certainly Alan is a snob and quite unlikable, but why the constant bickering? Why couldn't Rose Ann deal with the situation without William's having to hear daily reports on the feud?

Slowly William picks up the thread of conversation on the talk show that at the moment features a psychologist speaking about what seems to him to be an unending number of workshops on "human potential." William is vaguely amused by the discussion because he is certain that such workshops have little or no value—mere time-wasters. He feels about as mentally fit as anyone can be and he is certainly using his potential wisely. He is puzzled, however, by the ever-increasing need for other people to talk about their problems and become involved in therapy groups or other related activities. They tend to think too much about themselves, he believes. The psychologist now speaks of the need for her clients to learn to be open and real; in short, to be their true selves. William snorts. What else could one possibly be but oneself? Certainly each of us plays roles. William ticks off his own: husband, father, librarian, administrator, colleague, citizen. He acknowledges to himself that these are all necessary and real parts of himself. Then he hears the psychologist say something about using personal power, about the politics of self-awareness, and about choosing freely. Now that is more like it. William sighs to himself. If more people would recognize that they do have control over their lives, if they would be willing to make choices, to take responsibility for their behavior, then everyone would be better off. With that he reaches over and snaps off the set. Now if only Jonathan Thronly would stop playing games, he muses. . . .

Why set up an obviously successful administrator like William for an opening scene? Why limit his knowledge of himself and others? He could have been allowed to realize that he frequently plays another, relatively threatening role when he strategizes his financial dealings. He could have been allowed to see the connections between the conversations he heard on the talk show and the one he was having with himself. But William is portrayed here precisely because no matter who an individual is, no matter how successful, each person experiences difficulties in reaching out for more of his or her affective self. Many people, like William, feel perfectly comfortable with what they know about themselves and see no need to delve more deeply into their own feelings or attitudes. William, for instance, recognizes that other people have difficulties with communication but he, himself gifted and confident in so many ways, simply can see no connection between their problems and himself. It may seem, for instance, that Jonathan Thronly should retire quietly, with dignity, and without a board struggle. But to Thronly being chairman of the board may very well be the last, albeit tenuous, hold he has on his sense of pride and his sense of purpose in life itself. Rather than chance an unhappy disclosure of his feelings about retirement (and maybe even about death) with people who could be unresponsive and who might even resent him for bringing up such an unpleasant subject, Thronly engages in skillful avoidance of discussion on the matter of his retirement. Thronly's behavior William has labeled "playing games." William may well be avoiding his own true feelings and attitudes about aging and death. These feelings and attitudes may be prejudicing his evaluation of Thronly's performance as chairman of the board.

Obviously, the scene starring William is simplistic but is not entirely fictitious. Like William, a number of librarians are not necessarily convinced that self-knowledge, increased awareness of one's own feelings, and self-esteem have any real bearing on their professional performance or the performance of their colleagues or employees.

One of the authors has had experience with an experienced and respected administrator who feels that employees should be handled from a totally objective viewpoint, as pawns in the total strategy of library service. The strategist, from some remote pinnacle, is to figure out what is best for the overall library program and then to issue firm directives to bring about necessary changes. The administrator is not expected to be in communication with those who would be affected most by such decisions. There are no suggestions for involving the staff in problem-solving sessions. No democratic staff meetings, no vote, no possibility for consensus, no group process would be employed. The fate of the people involved is similar to professional sports wherein the players are bought and then sold if they do not perform as directed. The game, after all, is more important than the players.

Library literature has not yet gone beyond paying lip service to human problems. Even as admirable a work as Sullivan's *Problems in School Media Management* (1971) skirts the real problems lying behind the goal setting, the program design, the chain-of-command decision making so interestingly presented as management technique problems. In spite of the relatively realistic descriptions of personalities, power struggles, interpersonal and intrapersonal conflicts inevitably integral to such situations, nowhere does Sullivan encourage focusing on ways to process the feelings, attitudes, and values of the people as they interact with one another. Library/media science students, their professors and working librarians/media specialists are rarely professionally prepared to discuss or deal with the affective implications of the human relationships in such case studies. Through no fault of their own they have been shortchanged in their education, as have a great many other professionals who deal with people in their daily work. Better understanding of what motivates people to behave the way they do is needed. Some real insight into people's feelings, attitudes, and needs is necessary. Understanding and insight are dependent upon a degree of self-knowledge not emphasized in library schools or library literature.

Some Basic Tenets about Self

Many authors (e.g., Angyal, 1941; Maslow, 1968; White, 1959) describe in detail the basic need people have for a strong sense of self-worth. It is generally acknowledged that a person's sense of self-worth is constantly evolving and is a living entity that needs and seeks nourishment from the environment around it. People do not inherit a sense of self, but rather learn from their surroundings all the beliefs, attitudes, and feelings they have of themselves. All that they do, all that they are, and all that they may become depends on that sense of self-worth. It is therefore terribly important to recognize the impact of other human beings in life, since the ones who are closest to an individual (the significant others) provide that individual with the necessary nourishment or withhold that nourishment so essential to a sense of self esteem.

A second, equally crucial human need, then, is to be accepted, recognized, or needed by a "significant other," an important person or group of persons in someone's life (Angyal). The individual's sense of self worth is dependent upon this second need. The two together, called by Angyal "autonomy" and "homonomy," are the most important psychological building blocks in the development of all of the models of communication presented in this book. The title of this chapter signifies the paradoxical quality of these two basic needs. One really needs to love oneself in order to love one's neighbor; however, it is also true that one needs the neighbor's love to fully develop a personal sense of self-esteem, particularly when that neighbor is a "significant other" in an individual's life. People must also ask themselves the question, "Can I really love myself if I have not learned to love others?" It is a complex matter that does not lend itself to simplistic answers. Perhaps this is why so little has been done until recently to develop a psychology that deals with the affective domain.

Humanistic psychology directs itself toward changing the rather limited psychological view of self as an object or an animal to a view that the self is a special being with unique potential for actualization and personal growth. The tenets of humanistic psychology seek to augment and modify views of human behavior that have arisen from two basic schools of psychology, the Freudian and the Behaviorist. Both schools view human behavior as a reactive product. The Freudian school deals with instincts and with the unconscious and its influence on human behavior. Unconscious, instinctual demands, according to this school, impel a variety of behaviors designed to gratify and reduce internal stimulation. Specific behaviors and the general life style are overdetermined and permanently established by approximately age six. All subsequent human action is merely a compulsive repetition of these fixed patterns. Study of psychologically unsound personalities rather than mentally healthy subjects was the basis for the conclusions of this school. The Behaviorist school is interested in stimulus-response and associative learning. Here people are frequently compared with animals and are not always considered for their uniquely human characteristics.

The Humanistic approach is as much a philosophy as a methodology and stresses individuality, freedom, responsibility, and creativity as well as self-respect, love, and caring. Maslow spoke of humanistic psychology as the "third force" (distinguishing it from the other two schools), stating that it is the work of many people rather than characterized by and credited to the work of one person. Nevertheless many people consider that Maslow was the initial influence, the person who stimulated and gave strength to the beginnings of Humanistic psychology.

From the start Maslow objected to the study of human beings through the collection of statistical data. The Humanistic view looks to what people are capable of becoming; it emphasizes the positive, rather than accepting the present predictions of what is thought of as "normal" or average. Maslow also objected to the comparison made between animals and human beings. Too often these comparisons point out unfavorable or weak characteristics thought to be shared by animals and humans. Maslow pointed out that there are many unique human characteristics such as conscience, humor, art, patriotism, music, love, and self-sacrifice that cannot be compared to animal behavior and have therefore been left unstudied. Rodents and birds used for Behaviorist studies exhibited limited physiological instincts, and the resulting generalizations and assumptions made from such research tended to connect their primitive instincts to humans; humans therefore were labeled uncontrollable, powerful, and unmodifiable. Such conclusions are incomplete, incorrect, and limiting, according to Maslow, and do not take into consideration the hierarchy of human needs. Because human feelings, attitudes, and other affective reasons for behavior have not been the province of objective clinical research, they are thus ignored by scientists in the search for solutions to human problems.

Maslow and other Humanistic psychologists next turned to education as the most promising avenue to affect change. "Third Force psychological theory calls for a new kind of education . . . [with] more emphasis on development of the person's potential, particularly the potential to be human, to understand self and others and relate to them, to achieve basic human needs, to grow toward self-actualization" (Goble, 1970, p. 69).

Carl Rogers

A legend and reluctant guru to his many followers, Carl Rogers has maintained since the early 1940s that people are ultimately capable of solving their own problems and that counselors and psychotherapists too often inhibit rather than promote this capability. "I have a great deal of confidence in man's potential for resolving his own problems . . . but that confidence is based on the condition that the person is really aware of the facts. For example, in therapy, he becomes more and more aware of the inner facts about himself" (Rogers in Evans, 1975, p. 64).

Rogers visualized self-actualization as the process by which a person is "acceptantly aware of what's going on within and is consequently changing practically every moment and is moving on in complexity" (Evans, p. 17). For too long, Rogers maintained, therapists have kept people returning again and again for seemingly endless treatments, resulting in an overly dependent relationship upon the therapist. These sessions too often fail to solve the communications problems or the mental illness (neurosis or psychosis) of the individuals seeking help and become, in a sense, part of the problem or illness. In addition, this type of helping is generally expected to take years to accomplish and often costs many thousands of dollars, thus limiting the number of people who can afford treatment. Rogers also criticized the psychotherapist as a remote, uninvolved listener who shows little regard for the patient.

Based on his own experience, Rogers stated that an awareness and knowledge of the past are not as important as dealing with the present. For that reason he suggested that the helper step out of the way and allow the troubled person to help herself by experiencing the present and planning the future. (Instead of referring to her as a patient under someone's care, Rogers called her a client, someone who seeks help and who is in control. The person in the helping role Rogers called a "facilitator," rather than a counselor, analyst, or even teacher.) To reinforce the client's own power to help herself, Rogers placed only three major obligations upon a facilitator. "Those I have singled out as being essential are: a sensitive empathic understanding of the client's feelings and personal meanings; a warm acceptant prizing of the client and an unconditionality in this positive regard" (Evans, p. xxxi). Rogers stressed the need for a facilitator to be genuine when dealing with someone. In other words, if a facilitator is perceived as phony, deceptive, or dishonest, her relationship with a client can become further complicated, weakened, and inevitably less beneficial. Empathic understanding is an important component. The development of listening skills goes hand in hand with such empathy. For Rogers, however, that third ingredient (i.e., unconditional acceptance) is all-important. For the client to make progress she must perceive that the facilitator will continue to care for her no matter what feelings or behavior she may reveal in the course of their relationship together. And, although the client must take responsibility for changing her life for the better, she may well have previously lacked a positive model, someone who could offer her the nourishment needed from outside of herself to help her begin to build a positive self-image.

For the client, the journey to self-awareness may have many stumbling blocks. Rogers maintained that all people endeavor to preserve the concept or picture that they have of themselves and that "a sharp change in that picture is quite threatening" (Evans, p. 17). People apparently disregard knowledge of the self, behavior, feelings, and attitudes that might destroy the picture they already have of themselves (this includes both positive and negative knowledge). Incongruence usually results when an individual's experience contradicts her self-concept. An individual's self-concept may have been formed through early experiences with a "significant other," probably a mother or a father whose regard for the child was conditional upon certain behaviors. The individual, then, grows up thinking of herself as prized only under certain conditions. Again these may not be positive conditions. If, for instance, a person who comes from a deprived background does not readily respond to positive benefits or to attention, well-meaning individuals may misinterpret the response to their kindness. Being valued only under specific conditions may, in fact, induce desired behavior only under those conditions. That person's character may remain unaffected outside the area where the expectations have been internalized.

Over the years the authors have heard school librarians bemoan the behavior of culturally/socially deprived students who worked in their libraries. These librarians complained that some of their work-study students lacked appreciation for the opportunities offered by the library experience. "With all the attention, with the risk we take hiring them, with all the caring and attention paid, how could Noah pad his time sheet, how could Stephanie have stolen from the fine money, how could Louise still use that obscene language so carelessly?" Rogers's answer to those questions, in part, might be that they have poor self-images developed to a great degree from the early "conditional prizing" of their parents, and that they do not really see themselves necessarily as honest, responsible, or considerate. Thus they behave in dishonest, irresponsible, and nonconsiderate ways. The sympathy, patience, or generosity offered them by the librarian is not necessarily enough to change such behavior. Perhaps to expect a librarian to develop unconditional positive regard for her staff and for colleagues, as well as for the many people who use the library, is to ask the impossible. But remember that positive regard does not mean toleration or acceptance of deplorable or inappropriate behavior; it does mean that the person continues to care for an individual even while rejecting her unacceptable behavior, and that the caring is perceived and understood to be unconditional.

Two examples are in order here. Although neither of them have happy endings they illustrate that librarians should be aware of the importance of Roger's concept of unconditional prizing. The first involves a young man, Nathan, who was found to be padding his library time sheet. He had a long history of shoplifting and was on probation when he was hired by the library. The librarian understood that Nathan was gifted and intelligent and, if given a chance, might redeem himself and go on to lead a productive and happy life. She had spoken with his guidance counselor and his foster parents, all of whom were trying hard to give him the support he needed to make good. The librarian genuinely liked Nathan. When he was found padding his time sheet he had been working in the library for over a year. He had worked well and understood that he was liked personally in spite of his past history. The librarian confronted him with his dishonesty and expressed her disappointment. He explained that he was sorry, but only because he had been caught. The librarian replied that she felt she had been used, and that she was sorry he felt it necessary to try to "rip off" people who cared for him. He showed evidence of being highly uncomfortable with that information. She said that although she liked him a lot, she did not know how he could reestablish a sense of trust so that he could continue to work at the library. He responded that it was obvious that he could not pad his time sheet anymore, now that he had been caught. The librarian said that she did not know what else he might do, if all he cared about was whether or not he got caught. He had no answer to that. She then closed their discussion by telling him to think about the fact that she had no way of knowing how she could trust him unless he could prove it to her in some way. She left it that way, not firing him, but not inviting him to come back. This example has an open ending because the young man, at this writing, has not yet made a move to help solve his own problem.

The other example, also true, involves an incident that occurred when one of the authors stopped at the office of an assistant director of a large library system. While chatting about several professional matters of mutual interest, the director expressed her concern over one of her employees who had once worked for the author and who was also her personal friend. She asked the author what she thought she could do about this librarian's absenteeism. The author asked if the director had inquired as to why the librarian had been out so much; she replied that he had taken all of his sick leave and that she had inquired as to his health whenever he returned, which was infrequently. Apparently he gave rather vague answers that left the director uncertain as to what was really wrong. The author expressed her concern about his health, but even as she did so she saw that the director's thoughts were already turning elsewhere. She did not appear to be really interested in what the author had to say.

Later, as the author was leaving the building, she glanced into the office where the librarian in question had his desk. When he looked up from his work he signaled for her to come in and sit for a moment. Since they had known each other for years, they were happy for an opportunity to catch up on events. After they had exchanged brief news of friends and relatives, she asked him about his health. He seemed anxious to tell her about a severe bout with the flu that had left him depressed and in a weakened physical state. For weeks no amount of rest had seemed to help him catch up to his previous level of energy. He was not a young man and as he talked the author could see that he had been really frightened, that it was perhaps the closest he had ever been to death. Why, she wondered, had his employer not known how serious his illness had been and how depressed and anxious it had left him?

The author left the office not too long afterward feeling that her friend was certainly sounding pretty much in control of both his mental and his physical health, quite confident of complete recovery although he still tired easily. Before she left, however, she asked him if he had ever discussed his health with the director. "Not really. She means well, I guess," he said, "but she's not really interested in me. She has her special friends among the librarians in this building, you know, the younger set, but I'm not really one of them." In his own way he had discovered what the author knew as well. The director really did not care. Too bad, she thought. It should not have to be that way.

To sum up, Rogers viewed his work and his philosophy as educational, and the end result as "the facilitation of learning as the function which may hold constructive, tentative, changing process answers to some of the deepest perplexities which beset man today" (Rogers, 1975, p. 1). He also saw that a kind of social revolution was occurring as more and more people become caring facilitators who can offer unconditional positive regard to the people closest to them in their work, as well as in their families. He interpreted this as a kind of personal power. He spoke of the politics of self-awareness arising in a more person-centered world. Such a world would move toward non-defensive openness "within the family, the working task force, the system of leadership" (Rogers, 1977, p. 282).

Richard Farson credits Carl Rogers's work as "basic to the restructuring of almost every field of human affairs" (Evans, p. xxxix). Among the areas that Farson saw as influenced by a Rogerian approach were student-centered teaching and student's rights; lay and peer counseling; health and welfare programs that emphasize self-help groups; the involvement of citizens in planning for change in their communities; and child-rearing and children's rights. In addition he stated, "There has probably not been a single organizational development or management training program in 25 years which has not been built on his theoretical formulations" (Evans, p. xi).

From a librarian's point of view, all kinds of connections to the above paragraph can be noted. Certainly increasing numbers of citizens are deciding that they want to have a voice in what happens in their libraries. Certainly management procedures in industry have some parallels to library management. And certainly when human beings interact in the library there are individual rights and self-esteem to be considered on all sides.

It appears to be a relatively simple matter for the librarian to focus on the various normal interpersonal interactions that take place in the library or media center during the course of the working hours. In so doing it is also a simple matter to examine how Rogers's requirements for a facilitator (one who is genuine, who makes things easier, and who helps people function more easily and successfully) could fit into the scheme of things. How openness and genuineness, rather than fake cordiality or phoniness, make ultimate good sense in dealing with people. The librarian might feel that any problems might be handled with the relatively available avenues of courtesy and common sense, but both frequently evolve out of empathic feelings and a genuine regard for others, so there is already a good foundation on which to build even more successful communication skills.

The examples in this chapter have involved administrators dealing with employees with particularly human problems. There are, of course, human problems beyond the scope of the librarian's expertise, some of which may impose themselves, like it or not, on the library. Knowing when to call for help, when to refer troubled people for attention elsewhere, is also important. The librarian may experience extreme difficulties in dealing with distressed, angry, or even deranged individuals who enter the library and act out in unexpected and unacceptable ways. Carol Easton (1977, pp. 484–88) discussed this phenomenon, quoting one librarian who agreed that training in helping librarians deal with such individuals would be helpful, but that the library had no money for such a program. If, as Easton stated, the problem patron has been the profession's skeleton in the closet, librarians should then be prepared for this, as well as for normal interactions.

The Hidden Curriculum and the Written Curriculum

Listen to the salutation of the dawn
Look to this day
for it is life
the very life of life
In its brief course lie all
the realities and truths of existence
the joy of growth
the splendor of action
the glory of power
For yesterday is but a memory
And tomorrow is only a vision
But today well lived
makes every yesterday a memory of happiness
and every tomorrow a vision of hope
Look well therefore to this day!
—ancient Sanskrit poem

Another major approach to developing self-awareness evolved out of the classic psychology of Fritz Perls, whose major work was also published in the mid-twentieth century. Like that of Rogers, his work has had considerable impact on the directions of group and individual therapy, as well as in education, where it focuses on "the hidden curriculum." This section will deal with the significance of Gestalt education. The principles applied to the learner/facilitator situation show some interesting parallels to Rogers's way of thinking. There is, however, at least one significant difference. The Gestalt method is concisely directive; this Rogers would never approve. Gestalt techniques are equally as controversial as the Rogerian method, if not more so. The hidden curriculum is the personality and skills of any facilitator. Teachers and librarians model attitudes and values, as well as present ideas, skills, and content material. Thus, the hidden curriculum is "the frequently unstudied, informal, and concomitant learnings . . . that are provided through the teacher's behavior, the classroom norms, the interaction between teacher and student and among students, etc." (Phillips, 1976, p. 86).

Several goals are important when viewing the hidden curriculum. Taken directly from Gestalt counseling, these include:

1. Development of whole, integrated individuals whose thoughts, feelings, and actions occur to their fullest, congruent, and real potential.
2. Development of responsible individuals who are alive, sensitive, and in charge of, responsible for, and accountable for their lives.
3. Development of aware individuals who are fully in touch with themselves, with others, and with the world around them.
4. Development of individuals who are able to attend to the immediate present, the "here and now."
5. Development of nonmanipulative individuals who do not use others.

All facilitators must be complete if they hope to develop such completeness in their learners. Modeling these vital components within the context of the hidden curriculum is crucial if learners are to learn them. Indeed learners learn their facilitators.

Several initial studies (Miller and Kriegel, 1973; Phillips and Elmore, 1974; and Shifflett and Brown, 1972) of teacher training using Gestalt techniques have demonstrated significant increases and notable effects on teachers' personalities and on corresponding classroom behaviors.

Teaching skills associated with Gestalt techniques are direct spin-offs from changes in personalities and facilitator behaviors. Phillips (1976) listed seven:

1. The ability to differentiate one's own needs and concerns from those of the others. That is, to be able to recognize differences.
2. The ability to identify events at the moment, in the "here and now." That is, to not contaminate the immediate with past memories or future dreams.

3. The ability to use concise, correct, and courageous language. For example, using "I" rather than "one" or "we" allows both facilitator and, concomitantly, learners to take responsibility for their statements. Similarly, using "you" rather than "we" or "someone" makes communications personal and direct. Likewise, understanding the difference between and appropriately using "can't" and "won't" facilitates being responsible for feelings and behavior.

4. The use of friendly frustration. That is, to not do for learners what they can do or learn to do for themselves. Thus, learners are required to mobilize their resources to learn, to master, and to change.

5. Making the implicit explicit. Through explication, the facilitator can help make implicit assumptions and behaviors more open so that learners can see just what it is they are doing, how they are doing it, and what and how they are learning. For example, if a memory or a feeling is interfering in an individual's learning, the facilitator might ask the following questions: "What are you feeling now?" "Have you felt that before?" "When?" "How does that situation resemble this one?" "What can we do about it?" Answering these gently asked questions can clear away memories or feelings that contaminate the "here and now" experience and open the way for a person to attend to the present task. Another example might make explication more explicit. If a behavior that is clearly harmful and unacceptable occurs, the facilitator might ask the following questions: "David, what are you doing?" "Nothing!" "What did you do to Frankie?" "Frankie's a creep!" "What did you do to Frankie?" "Aahh, hit him?" "Yes, now put that into a statement starting with the word 'I.'" After the student does this, the facilitator can turn to his counterpart and repeat the sequence. This nonpunitive, repetitive questioning facilitates learning willingness and ability to own feelings and behaviors, making them explicit and open rather than implicit and hidden.

6. Facilitating closure. In the two examples above, the facilitator is helping the students reach closure, is aiding them in finishing unfinished business. This skill closes the Gestalt, reestablishes balance, completes a cycle allowing students to move on to other things. Closure is important for class sessions, acts of learning, incidents between people, group work, or for a course. Finishing unfinished business allows facilitator and learner to move on

without carrying with them contamination that will interfere in future events.

7. Creating a climate that legitimizes the expression of feelings. Making feelings a part of the library or of the classroom gives them credibility and realness.

The second major focus of this model is on the written curriculum. Shifflett (1975) makes a strong case for using affective loadings to promote learning. These are the feelings and emotional reactions that accrue to all learning tasks. When used effectively they "enrich personal meaning, increase relevance, and broaden understanding" (p. 115). The use of affective loadings requires the facilitator to move away from the purely cognitive and toward affect and images.

Many Gestalt techniques (e.g., visualization, directed fantasy, internal dialogue, etc.) easily stimulate feelings and images. It is a simple step to target them toward a particular subject matter or lesson. For example, to enliven and enhance the discussion of slavery, a teacher might lead the class through a guided fantasy on a day in the life of a slave. Similarly, a reader's advisory librarian conducting a discussion on poetry might have participants close their eyes and attend to the feelings generated and visualize the images stimulated by the reading of a poem. Likewise, a graphics arts or audiovisual specialist might facilitate students' sensitivity to and perceptiveness of their surroundings by using an awareness scanning experiment. That is, students would be asked to slowly look around their immediate surroundings and write in the present tense what they are aware of (i.e., see, hear, feel, smell, etc.), making as complete a listing as they can.

If one aspect of learning is assumed to be personal and social development, the techniques can also be applied. The use of visualization and fantasy can help people become more aware of their typical emotional states and their emotional reactions to certain situations. Having them fantasize an animal that best represents them can be revealing regarding feelings about self. Expanding that fantasy to include the animal living in its natural environment and then confronting its natural enemy can provide information about hopes, fears, concerns, and styles of dealing with conflict or difficulties. Another example is to have students imagine that they are an animal that did not get on Noah's Ark and have them select a color that best expresses the way that animal might feel. This is particularly useful in teaching the relationship of color to mood, as well as helping students identify their typical emotional reaction to frustration and threat. If a person seems upset or out-of-sorts, one way to highlight and dramatically represent the feelings and possibly the causative factors is to have him come up with a book or movie title that best describes the situation in which he finds himself. Labeling the feelings and situation in this way can help the individual see the situation more clearly and find the possible outlets.

An important part of all learning is a set of process skills for developing alternatives and solving problems. Within this context Gestalt techniques are particularly salient. A singular assumption in this model is that solutions, like problems, lie within the person. A classic and potent procedure, then, is to put the problem-creator in contact with the problem-solver. Dialogue techniques can be used with personal problems, learning blocks, social issues, and other areas.

A facilitator might use the open-chair technique to facilitate learners' awareness of contemporary social issues. By having learners talk through both positions of a current critical social issue, for instance, they can both appreciate that many social issues cannot be cast into a right-or-wrong mode and so develop a clearer understanding of their own value positions. Advocacy librarians might use the technique to put people in touch with two sides of an issue. For example, alternately a woman and a man can act through a dialogue between Superman and Super-woman. Using a Top-dog/Under-dog dialogue might help a children's librarian clarify the message and the moral of a number of fairy tales and children's stories. What would have occurred, for example, in such a dialogue between Jack and the Giant or between Cinderella at home and Cinderella at the ball? A teacher might have a student recreate a dialogue between his diffident self and his all-knowing guru. In all the above examples problems are posed, analyzed, and alternative answers or understandings are developed.

In summary, essentially the Gestalt model seeks to make personal, relevant, and real any and all learning materials, whether personal, interpersonal, skill-oriented, content-focused, or value-issue related. It is designed to bridge the gaps between head and gut, thought and emotion, imagery and experience, fantasy and reality, and among people. The model constructs a series of linkages among thought, affect, and imagination. Valuing all three equally, it attempts to harness all three and fuse the creative, emotional, and cognitive within facilitator and learners in order to fully integrate these components into a working whole.

Negative Criticism

Critics, however, do not see the impact of Maslow, Rogers, or Perls from an optimistic viewpoint. Beyond the fact that these models are not considered viable replacements for psychotherapy or psychoanalysis by the practitioners of those treatments or techniques, some other problems are also evident. Criticism is leveled at psychotherapy itself; that is, only the rich or upper middle class can afford to be treated. Facilitating group sessions and individual therapy can be as costly as the more traditional forms of help. This model does not apply exclusively to therapy. There are a large number of public schools where teachers practice facilitating rather than lecturing or teaching in the traditional manner. In this way students are learning to help themselves become life-long learners, their own problem solvers and healers.

Another criticism contends that Maslow, Rogers, and those who follow Gestalt techniques have oversimplified therapy so much that many people with little or no training have become facilitators. To some of the Humanistic group this is the way it should be, but to others (the authors included) it seems a dangerous trend. Evidence indicates that a number of people have been severely distressed by becoming involved in such activities; such distress is doubtlessly related to inexperience rather than to the models. This assertion is unfortunately difficult to document.

In addition, awareness may cause more problems than it solves. Some people do not want to become more aware of their lives. To do so might be more painful than present existence. Like the proverbial opening of Pandora's box, for some people it may be better not to know. In other cases, people's level of awareness is at a perfectly comfortable level. They share of themselves with those closest to them and learn what they need to know about themselves in return. They are not involved in complicated social groups, they are not dealing with large numbers of people, and in a sense they are protected or sheltered from the complexities of human nature.

Another criticism deals with some serious distortions of theory that have developed. If Maslow, Rogers, and Perls have indeed demystified therapy, thereby making it more available for more people, it also follows that some of those people have distorted and misinterpreted even the most simple messages. For example, one of Rogers's weaknesses, according to Farson, is that he is unable to recognize either the complexity of human affairs or the coexistence of opposites. "His is essentially a linear theory, as opposed to a curvilinear one; maximizing rather than optimizing . . . 'the more the better' as opposed to 'there can be too much of a good thing!' " (Evans, p. xxxvii). One problem with this situation is that it tends to multiply itself with some of the followers. If, for instance, it is decided that it is beneficial for people to talk about their feelings, then the facilitator's function is to create a situation whereby the person will have to talk about her feelings. If she appears to have no feelings, then the facilitator should create a situation whereby feelings will be experienced, forced if necessary. If tears and screaming are evidence of feelings then the facilitator should, perhaps, encourage these expressions of emotion. Primal Therapy (Janov, 1971) is such a model. The facilitator becomes a controlling force and the client becomes subject to her will and whim. All of which is far afield from anything Maslow or Rogers would wish for. It is, however, the route that Gestalt therapy has taken.

Perhaps the most serious criticism holds that Rogers's method as a treatment for disturbed individuals is no treatment at all and that it does not work. This criticism appears to be incorrect, since a number of studies have shown that the method as described above is most effective in helping significant numbers of people to help themselves (Rogers and Dymond, 1954). Some critics persist in stating that nothing works anyway for very long, not therapy, not even religion. Evans would reply to them that the outcome of interactions is not what counts. Rogers provided a process, a way of being with one another that is ethical, democratic, and that helps people maintain their individuality and sense of dignity as persons. He made it clear that people need not feel powerless and that they can take control over their lives. If this message is understood and interpreted correctly, it can hardly be faulted.

One criticism, however, relates to the philosophy of all these models. People sometimes use self-awareness techniques as an escape from responsibility; knowingly or unknowingly they may be using it as a kind of social "cop-out." Too much self-absorption may prevent them from dealing with the major problems and social ills that are the real threat to humanity. It does no good for the poor, for racial minorities, women, homosexuals, or others who have been oppressed to become overly engaged in self-study or contemplation. There must be group action and social organization to correct the prejudices and injustices of the world. "Oppression is not simply a matter of certain individuals behaving in unloving or unliberated ways. It is systematic, socially structured and culturally reinforced. To understand and change it, we usually will need to focus on a great many sociocultural factors—ranging from economic structure to the mass media, from status hierarchies to the legal system, from employment opportunities to childrearing attitudes. When problems transcend the personal or interpersonal levels, so too must the solutions. This is perfectly clear to the black unable to find a job, or the woman denied a legal abortion. In such situations no amount of self awareness will suffice" (Schur, 1976, pp. 4–5).

I do my thing, and you do your thing.
I am not in this world to live up to your expectations
And you are not in this world to live up to mine.
You are you and I am I
And if by chance we find each other
It is beautiful.

                              —Fritz Perls

              The Getsmart Prayer*

I do my thing, and you do your thing.
I am not in this world to live up to your expectations
And you are not in this world to live up to mine.
You are you and I am I
And if by chance we find
Our brothers and sisters enslaved
And the world under fascist rule
Because we were doing our thing—
It can't be helped?

                    —with no apologies to Fritz Perls

A Model of Interpersonal Dynamics

To understand oneself means to some degree learning about oneself from others, sharing more of oneself with others, and learning more about them as well. One way to describe the sharing process involved is through the Johari window (Luft, 1969). A concept developed by Joseph Luft and Harry Ingham, it is a set of squares used to diagram the process of communication between individuals. The Johari window can be seen in figure 2.

Square No. 1 shows that area about the person known both to her and to others.	1. Open	2. Blind	Square No. 2 is that area that the person does not know about herself but is known to others.
Square No. 3 is that area that is known only by the person and not by others.	3. Hidden	4. Unknown to Anyone	Square No. 4 is that area that is unknown to anyone, lying within the unconscious mind of the individual.

Figure 2. The Johari Window

* Reprinted with permission from *Rough Times*, *3*, no. 3 (Dec. 1972). Copyright 1972 by the R. T. Collective.

Luft explained the squares by saying "1. The smaller the first quarter the poorer the communication. 2. Threat tends to decrease awareness. Mutual trust tends to increase awareness. 3. A change in any quadrant of the window will affect all other quadrants" (Luft, 1969, p. 14).

Luft urged that people look at the window in terms of shared knowledge. If a person is unknown to another individual, the first quadrant of her window will be very small in her relationship with the observer. It will be difficult for that person to talk with her effectively. As the people work together, however, they will share information about themselves; thus there will be less of the hidden and blind areas in each Johari window. The observer will enlarge the open areas that both share. It will then be easier to communicate, and as each trusts the other with information, they will increase their awareness of each other as individuals.

In the Johari window, square number two can be increased by the use of feedback. Similar to looking in a mirror or using videotape, feedback can be powerful and painful for an individual, but it also promotes growth and understanding. According to Luft (1969) there are five varieties of feedback that can be applied to the Johari window. The first way, called "information," paraphrases what has just been said. It is not unlike the type of questioning techniques recommended by Gordon (1975) when he suggested that one individual may help another clarify how she is feeling about a problem simply by paraphrasing what was said, rather than offering any personal solutions. A person receiving feedback in this way can then determine whether she should modify or confirm what others have just told her about what she has said or done.

The second way, "personal" feedback, is also similar to Gordon's technique for problem solving (for the person who "owns" the problem, in this case); it involves the expression of personal feeling about what someone has just said or done. "When you said that I felt. . . ." This is the type of reaction that can be painful and is often avoided because of fear of hurting the other person's feelings. If, however, it is worded carefully, as Gordon suggests, with concern for the other, and if it remains an "I" rather than an accusatory "you" statement, it may not be so difficult for the other person to handle. This situation allows someone to learn more about how an individual is feeling without becoming a blamer or an accuser.

A "judgmental" reaction, on the other hand, is one in which, according to Luft, the speaker offers an opinion about what she has just heard or seen. This kind of feedback is not generally acceptable or helpful and may cause the receiver to put up barriers against the person offering such critical commentary. As Gordon has stated, if a person's opinion is to have real value, she must be "hired" as an expert. Then, when asked, the other person needing feedback is expecting the judgment to be sound and of value.

An even stronger version of this kind of feedback was characterized by Luft as "forced" and is not recommended because it deliberately calls attention to a person's blind area, the part of her Johari window that she cannot see herself. In forced feedback, the receiver is apt to hear, "Can't you see what you have done . . . ?"

The fifth form of feedback Luft calls "interpretation," which he considered to be a variation of forced feedback, but which has a more complex approach in that the giver is likely to explain in detail why she thinks certain things were said or done. This may be done with the best of intentions but with poor timing or poor understanding of the total picture, and will probably not add much insight or increased knowledge between the two people involved. Luft called attention to feelings of defensiveness that may arise in this kind of feedback when he referred to Gibb's (1968) description of six defensive behaviors: evaluation, control, strategy, neutrality, superiority, and certainty. Luft included these defensive behaviors as a reminder of how easily people can close off communication without realizing it. He stressed what Gibb called supportive climates, which are the opposites of the above six: description, problem-orientation, spontaneity, empathy, equality, and provisionalism.

A way of providing more growth and an increase in the sharing of the hidden area, number three, of the Johari window involves a willingness on the individual's part to disclose information about herself that is unknown to others. Trust is a key factor here, and it is often difficult for a person to determine how much is too much, as well as how little is not enough. According to Luft, self-disclosure is appropriate when there is an on-going relationship and the act of self-disclosure is not simply a random activity; when there is reciprocity and a feeling of interdependency and mutual involvement; when the time is right; when self-disclosure is appropriate to what is happening and people's feelings are taken into account; when disclosure will not radically alter the relationship; when parties involved are both aware of how disclosure is affecting each of them; when there is a reasonable risk involved, not one that will leave the participants totally unprepared for what may follow; when there is a crisis and a real need to reveal important information to allow for healing or rekindling of an important relationship; and finally when the participants have enough in common to fully understand and appreciate what self-disclosure will do to their relationship.

The 100 Books: A Case Study

Librarians are sometimes faced with awkward situations in which well-meaning persons offer inappropriate advice, services, or gifts to the library. A simple statement clearly describing library policy takes care of most such situations, but a certain number may escalate into uncomfortable and unhappy consequences for all involved.

Such an incident actually occurred when a school librarian was presented with 100 books by an individual of a particular religious persuasion.

The authors share it here not because the resolution was the perfect answer, but rather because a humanistic approach to the problem was used when policy was questioned. It exemplifies the need for confluent thinking, a blending of the cognitive aspects of librarianship, as well as an affective awareness of the human situation, the human needs. One without the other would not have worked.

In an average-sized urban high school with a fine media center, Jill Morris directs a library program funded with a good budget. She is able to provide the appropriate number of books and other media to meet the needs of the curriculum. In addition she has been able to provide her young adult readers with a wide selection of popular paperbacks that are frequently recommended by the teachers for pleasure reading.

During the school year she is approached by Mrs. Arlene Bowen, who wishes to present the library with 100 religious books. She informs Jill that these books make good "popular reading" and that they are not books of a particular sect. Jill expresses interest in the books and asks Mrs. Bowen to bring them in so that she may evaluate them. She explains the school's selection policy, and also explains that the school board delegates authority for selection of materials to her and her staff. For a book to be purchased it is generally recommended by a member of the faculty or the student body. It must also be checked with guidelines and book selection sources commonly used by professional librarians. The guidelines she uses for selection of material are also included as part of school board policy. After explaining all of this she tells Mrs. Bowen that any books that fit the criteria will be accepted; all others will be returned.

After examination of the books it is found that only two of the books are appropriate for the collection. When Mrs. Bowen is informed of this fact she is quite indignant. She reminds the librarian that she noticed several titles in the paperback section when she first entered the media center. She also remembers that *Soul on Ice* happens to be prominently displayed. Jill feels a bit uncomfortable and wonders momentarily if it wouldn't be easier just to accept the books and dispose of them without bothering to let the woman know. She knows of several librarians who take care of unwanted gifts in just this way.

It appears, however, that Mrs. Bowen has accepted her explanation and is going to take her books elsewhere. She explains that many other libraries have already accepted the books and are grateful to have them. Jill feels a bit defensive. She is tempted to reveal what some librarians actually do with unwanted material, but then realizes that some librarians actually do consider this material appropriate. Instead, she quietly thanks the woman for thinking of the school library even if things didn't work out.

Two weeks later, when the superintendent is discussing other matters with Jill, he mentions that Mrs. Bowen has been by to see him. "She'll be back to see you one of these days," he says casually. Jill responds by saying that she doesn't see why that should be necessary; he has explained the board policy to the woman, hasn't he? Well, yes, but he doesn't see that these particular books are all that objectionable, so he thinks he will let her handle the matter. Hiding her disappointment in his lack of support and his bypassing of board policy, she realizes that she will have to confront Mrs. Bowen at least one more time. This time it will be considerably more difficult.

Before Mrs. Bowen arrives Jill prepares herself for an unpleasant situation. She feels personally involved now, much more so than when she believed she had the backing of an administrator. She realizes that the superintendent really expects her to take the books. He is not so concerned with what she might do with them later, as long as she doesn't upset Mrs. Bowen. She understands that he has to confront various irate parents and citizens in all kinds of situations all day long, and that he must tire of being on the front line, the receiving end, but she is feeling defensive and resents his "passing the buck" to her.

She also realizes that Mrs. Bowen must by now have identified her as the culprit. The superintendent has, without saying so, indicated that Jill is the one to blame if the books don't get on the shelves. Up to this point Jill has been reacting. She has not given a thought for Mrs. Bowen, except as her antagonist. Now, however, she begins to see Mrs. Bowen, as a person with a purpose, someone who truly believes that what she is doing is needed in society. Just as Jill thinks of her library work as significant, Mrs. Bowen sees her mission as helping people through the books they read. Of course there are differences in their philosophies and approaches, but there is something basic with which Jill can empathize.

By the time Mrs. Bowen arrives, Jill's frame of mind is more comfortable. She invites her to come in and sit down in a small conference room where they can talk without interruption. Mrs. Bowen explains crisply that the superintendent has informed her that he will allow Jill to decide about the books. He has told her that he sees no harm in the books being present in the school. Mrs. Bowen suggests several ways in which the books might be shelved, separately or within the collection. Jill explains that shelf room is not the only issue.

Then she does something she has not done before with Mrs. Bowen. She becomes personal. She tells her in a kindly way how she understands that for Mrs. Bowen the gift of these books to the library is very important in her work. She waits while Mrs. Bowen confirms this fact and explains her religious beliefs in some detail. When Mrs. Bowen finishes Jill asks her if she can perhaps understand Jill's position, that she truly feels she must live with the board policy—to carry out policy. The selection policy discourages purchase or acceptance of most religious books because of their proselytizing nature. Step by step she takes Mrs. Bowen through the logic of the policy, giving her examples of other religious groups who have also attempted and failed to place their books in the library. She does all this with gentleness and compassion. She says that she knows it is very hard for Mrs. Bowen to accept this decision. Then she shares her insight into the similarities of both of their positions. Both want to help people through their reading. Both want a better world. Each pursues her cause in a different way. It is a sensitive moment. If Jill does not believe her own words, if she fakes sincerity and is simply using Mrs. Bowen to find a way out of an uncomfortable situation, this would be the worst kind of dissemblance and hypocrisy.

Instead she finds that she is capable of genuine concern for Mrs. Bowen. Mrs. Bowen senses that Jill does care. She softens visibly. It becomes possible for her to acknowledge that Jill, too, has a job to do. For a brief moment they eye each other acknowledging and reinforcing each other's point of view. Jill reaches out and shakes Mrs. Bowen's hand, thanking her once again, this time not only for having wanted to contribute to the library but for her gracious acceptance of Jill's position. She hastens to assure Mrs. Bowen that if there are other books she would like the library to consider to send them along. Mrs. Bowen eagerly places the school library on her mailing list and promises to send a few titles in the near future.

While it is more than obvious that any courteous librarian might have followed the same steps and successfully reached a happy conclusion, would such a librarian also have understood why her courtesy worked and how she could employ her skills again to avoid other unpleasant confrontations? Remember that not all situations work out as well. There are times when the librarian justifiably, but regrettably, feels so threatened that her sense of courtesy deserts her, or seems to be of little value. In such a situation, if she has some understanding of her own reactions and the reactions of others, if she can give her feelings some expression within a controlled situation, and if she can allow some empathy for her protagonist, a resolution may be possible with a minimum of discomfort on both sides. Needless to say the public relations of the library as well as the integrity of the librarian are both at stake.

AN EXERCISE

Detecting Defensive Behaviors

Referring to Gibb's six defensive behaviors—evaluation, control, strategy, neutrality, superiority and certainty, see if you can recognize which kinds of behavior are at work in the following statements. See also if you can find their opposites (i.e., problem-orientation, description, empathy, equality, provisionalism and spontaneity) in some of the other statements also listed below.

1. Look, you've got to slow down. The quality of what you are doing is suffering because you push yourself far too much for your age. I should probably reassign you to a less busy branch.
2. I know you feel uncomfortable about working in this department. It isn't easy to switch from one job to another so entirely new and different. Is there some way I can help you fit in with us more happily?
3. We need to work on ways to improve our public relations with the business community. Any ideas?
4. I understand, I hear what you're saying; but I hear the same thing from other librarians in this building too. Everybody has her share of problems. Now me, for instance. . . .
5. I'm sorry, we are really looking for a male librarian who can handle a relatively rough neighborhood. Wouldn't you feel frightened about driving a bookmobile into ghetto areas?
6. In the past I've solved the same kind of problem that you seem to be having now by readjusting my work schedule. We all take on more than we can handle sometimes. How about asking Marcia if she has time to give you a little help?
7. Some of these subject headings don't really reflect the needs of the people who use the library. Is there some way we might find to insert some of the newer words that our young people just

naturally use when referring to the subjects that interest them?
For example. . . .

8. I'm one of the top acquisitions librarians in this country. There
   are only a handful of us who really know the field!

9. I'm sure this is the only source you should use. You've been
   looking in all the wrong places again.

10. The library is changing directions as far as our outreach program
    is concerned. Your department will now be responsible for taking
    care of all the things described in the plan that the board, the
    director, and I have just completed.

11. I have watched you working with various elderly people. They
    seem hesitant to sit down when they are at your desk discussing
    their reading needs and asking for help. Is there some way you
    might find to help them relax a little bit as they talk with you?

12. You are paid by the hour, and a half hour is all the library is
    going to give you for lunch time. Sorry.

13. This bibliography is simply not typed correctly. You've been
    told so many times I don't know what else to say. Can't you see
    your own mistakes?

14. I can't really imagine why we should meet with the librarians
    who work in ———. We have nothing in common.

References

Angyal, Andras. *Foundations for a science of personality.* New York:
Commonwealth Fund, 1941.

Easton, Carol. Sex and violence in the library: Scream a little louder,
please. *American Libraries,* 1977, *8,* 484–88.

Evans, Richard I. *Carl Rogers: The man and his ideas.* New York:
Dutton, 1975.

Gibb, Jack. Defensive communication. In Warren Bennis, et al. (eds.),
Interpersonal Dynamics. Homewood, Ill.: The Dorsey Press, 1968.

Goble, Frank G. *Third force: The psychology of Abraham Maslow.* New
York: Viking, 1970.

Gordon, Thomas. *Teacher effectiveness training.* New York: Wyden,
1975.

Hall, C. S., and Lindzey, G. *Theories of personality.* 3d ed. New York:
Wiley, 1977.

Janov, Arthur. *The primal scream.* New York: Dell, 1971.

Luft, Joseph. *Group processes.* Palo Alto, Calif.: Mayfield Pub., 1969.

———. *Of human interaction.* Palo Alto, Calif.: Mayfield Pub., 1969.

Maslow, Abraham H. *Toward a psychology of being.* New York: Van
Nostrand, 1968.

Miller, S., and Kriegel, M. *The Ford-Esalen project in confluent education: End of year report 1972–1973.* Santa Barbara, Calif.: DRICE, 1973.

Phillips, Mark. The application of Gestalt principles in classroom teaching. *Group & organization studies*, 1976, *1*, 82–98.

———, and Elmore, B. *Follow-up report on DRICE participants*, 1974. Santa Barbara, Calif.: DRICE, 1974.

Rogers, Carl R. *Carl Rogers on personal power.* New York: Delacorte, 1977.

———. In Donald A. Read and Sidney B. Simon (eds.), *Humanistic education sourcebook*, 1–19. Englewood Cliffs, N.J.: Prentice-Hall, 1975.

———, and Dymond, R. F. *Psychotherapy and personality change.* Chicago: University of Chicago Press, 1954.

———, Gendlin, G. T., Kiesler, D. V., and Truax, C. B. *The therapeutic relationship and its impact: A study of psychotherapy with schizophrenics.* Madison: University of Wisconsin Press, 1967.

Schur, Edwin M. *The awareness trap.* New York: McGraw-Hill, 1976.

Shifflett, J. Beyond vibration teaching: Research and development in confluent education. In George Isaac Brown (ed.), *The live classroom.* New York: Viking, 1975.

———, and Brown, George Isaac. *Confluent education: Attitudinal and behavioral consequences of confluent teacher training.* University Center, Mich.: University Center Monograph Series, 1972.

Sullivan, Peggy. *Problems in school media management.* New York: R. R. Bowker Co., 1971.

Truax, C. B., and Carkhuff, R. R. *Toward effective counseling and psychotherapy: Training and practice.* Chicago: Aldine, 1967.

White, Robert W. Motivation reconsidered: The concept of competence. *Psychological Review*, 1959, *66*, 297–333.

7 Problem Formation and Solution

Some Approaches and Strategies

The Scene: A large, gothic-looking reading room in a university library at closing time. Leslie Lawrence, the student coordinator for the university's degree program, is checking the various cubicles for materials and/or students still cramming for that last, little bit of information for the next day's examinations. As she approaches the farthest cubicle, she hears a faint and muffled crying. She comes upon a young woman whose head is in her arms on the desk top. She is sobbing quietly. Leslie is hesitant, unsure what to do. Slowly and gingerly, she approaches the woman. As if aware of the presence of another person, the woman snaps upright and glares through tear-filled eyes at Leslie. As Leslie gropes for words, the woman gets up and rushes past her. It is only after she has passed that Leslie realizes who she is.

Later, sitting in her apartment, Leslie recalls seeing the student a number of times, always in similar moods in the same situation. The student always arrived in the reading room shortly after five P.M. and remained until closing time. More important, Leslie remembers that she apparently never sat with or talked with other people. In fact, Leslie remembers in the past noticing that the student appeared to be extremely cautious, if not frightened, around others. In spite of feeling uneasy, Leslie is concerned about the event that has just transpired.

The next evening Leslie attempts to find the student and resolves to spend a little time with her. But the student is nowhere to be found.

Several days go by and Leslie still cannot turn up this enigmatic woman. Other staff members either do not know who Leslie is talking about or can only vaguely recollect such a person. As time passes, other people and other events gradually move in to take their place in Leslie's thoughts.

About a month later, again at closing time, Leslie comes upon the woman. She looks sad-faced but at least is not tearful. Leslie asks if they might talk. Somewhat suspiciously the young woman agrees. Uncertainly, Leslie leads her to the front lounge. They sit. For what seems an awkward eternity they remain quiet. Now that they are sitting across from each other, neither appears to know what to say or why they are together. Finally Leslie says, "You are obviously upset about something. When I'm upset, sometimes I meditate. Sometimes I go to my counselor for help. You really should do something." The woman does not respond. She becomes more nervous, fidgeting and glancing furtively about the lounge. Tears well in the young woman's eyes. She springs up and runs out of the library. It is only after she is gone that Leslie realizes she never asked her name. Leslie never saw the young woman again. She had not discovered who she was, what was troubling her, or whatever happened.

Help . . . what a word! Help indicates that an individual has a problem or problems. Help points to the fact that a person has run out of alternatives to deal with the circumstance or a set of circumstances. Help means that past methods of coping are temporarily ineffective. *The Random House College Dictionary* provides sixteen definitions of the word help. These range from "to cooperate effectively with" through "to be of service or advantage" or "to save; rescue; succor" (1973, p. 16). It is, however, what the word implies that gives pause and great difficulty. By and large needing help implies failure, weakness, and inadequacy. Because these implications cut across many areas (i.e., technical assistance, aid in finding materials, help with interpersonal difficulties, and so forth), people have difficulty seeking, asking for, and using help in a number of situations. That certainly was the case with the young woman mentioned above.

From time to time everyone needs help; all face problems at certain times in their lives. At these times, once people have dealt with the implications noted above, they seek out someone to help. More often than not they hope that that person's advice will take care of the problem. The person offering assistance also hopes that his advice will be useful. But is advice really help? Most people would probably answer yes. In many cases, however, another's advice is not useful because it presumes too much. Specifically, it presumes that the helper's needs, goals, feelings, skills, and satisfactions are equivalent to those of the help-seeker. Because people are different, this equivalency does not exist. Therefore, the helper's advice will only be useful for him when he confronts a similar problem. Chances are it will not be useful for the person presenting the problem.

The three helping or problem-solving models presented below do not use advice. They are designed to help the person seeking help to help himself, to solve his own problem. The models are: transactional analysis, effectiveness training, and reality therapy.

Transactional Analysis

The theoretical framework of transactional analysis (Berne, 1961) emphasizes four elements: (1) ego states (i.e., Parent, Adult, and Child); (2) transactions between people and among ego states; (3) an individual's existential position (i.e., the health of self and others); and (4) a person's preconscious life-plan or script.

Ego states represent habitual ways of thinking, feeling, and reacting that occur together. Berne (1961, 1964) stated that all people have and experience the three ego states. The pattern of ego state operation is variable. At times the Parent is operating, at other times the Adult, and at still other times the Child is operating. Each ego state comes into focus depending on the situation in which and on the people with which the person finds himself.

The Parent feels, thinks, and behaves in the same ways as an individual's natural parents did. The functions of the Parent that are grouped under either the Critical Parent or the Nurturing Parent include limit-setting, disciplining, protecting, teaching, rule-making, keeping traditions, nurturing, judging, advising, and criticizing. The Adult is the thinking and information-processing ego state. It is the part of the person that stores memories, computes, gathers data, explores alternatives, makes plans and decisions, and calculates. It is the cool, dispassionate fact-finder. The Child is the individual when young; the feelings, thoughts, and behaviors that this person had, experienced, and displayed while a chronological child. The functions of the child grouped under the Adapted Child are angry, frustrated, rebellious, frightened and conforming aspects; under the Natural Child they are composed of the spontaneous, creative, carefree, curious, loving, trusting, and adventurous aspects.

Although no ego state is considered better or more important than the other two, Anderson (1973) stressed the desirability of having the Adult functioning much of the time. Indeed it is the Adult that analyzes and solves problems. Neither the harsh, overprotective Parent nor the

petulant, fun-loving Child has the objectivity or critical introspective-
ness to formulate or resolve issues within a person or between people.

A transaction is either a verbal or a nonverbal communication
between two or more people. Transactions, which originate from any
of the three ego states, can be *parallel, crossed,* or *ulterior.* For example,
a parallel transaction can be adult-to-adult-to-adult.

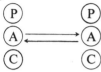 1. Could you tell me where I'd find *The Reader's
Guide to Periodical Literature?*
2. The indexes are located to your left at the
top of those stairs.

A parallel transaction can also be parent-to-child-to-parent:

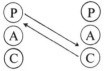 1. How many times have I told you to put the
books back on the shelves when you're
finished?
2. These aren't mine, honest. They're Jimmy's!

The crucial aspects of a parallel transaction are that the return message
originates from the ego state toward which the first message is directed
and that it is directed toward the ego state from which the original
message comes.

A crossed transaction occurs when the return message originates
from a different ego state than the one toward which the first message
is intended and when it is directed toward an ego state other than the
one from which the first message comes:

 1. Is the microfilm reader turned off?
2. Why do you always assume that I never turn
anything off?

Or:

 1. How many times have I told you to return
the books to the shelves when you're finished?
2. By my estimate, 37 times.

Typically, a crossed transaction brings both parties up short and puts
a temporary halt to further communication. By comparison, communication can continue indefinitely in parallel transactions.

In an ulterior transaction, a hidden message is directed toward an
ego state other than the one toward which the ostensible message is
directed:

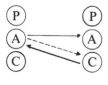 1. (A woman): Why don't we just continue
working on this section of the budget until
we're finished. (Somewhat flirtatiously): Then,
you can come over to my place for a late
supper.
2. (A man): (Somewhat interested): O.K.!

In this example, the woman disguises a seductive message to her younger male counterpart. He indicates a willingness to play whatever game she has in mind. It is the ulterior transaction that sets up a game sequence, the end result of which may lead to uncomfortable feelings for both players.

Two special types of transactional messages bear mentioning because of their importance to existential positions and scripts. These are *strokes* and *injunctions/counterinjunctions*. The former are the verbal or nonverbal recognitions of one's existence by another; the touches, smiles, hugs, hellos, spankings, slaps, punches, angry words, expressions of gratitude and encouragement, words of anger and dismay. Berne (1961, 1964) argued that both the symbolic-word and the physical strokes are vital for physical and emotional well-being. Strokes come in four varieties. *Positive strokes* convey a feeling of "you count." *Negative strokes* convey a feeling of "you do not count." *Conditional strokes* are those given for another's doing something. *Unconditional strokes* are those given for another's being, just because the other exists.

Injunctions are feeling messages—fears, wishes, desires, anger—that natural parents felt prohibited or inhibited about when they were children. These are located in the Parent ego states, but are preverbally or nonverbally expressed with irrational intensity by the angry or frightened Child ego state. Below are several examples of injunctions that typically take a "don't" form: Don't grow up! Don't be well, be sick! Don't be close! Don't be you, be me or someone else! Don't make it! Don't feel! Don't think! Don't be! Coexisting with these irrational "orders" are the counterinjunctions. These are the slogans related to expected and/or acceptable behavior. Several examples of counterinjunctions that typically take a "do" form are: Grow up! Be perfect! Try harder! Please me! Always do it yourself! Pull yourself up by your own bootstraps!

Strokes, injunctions, and counterinjunctions play vital roles in any person's selection of a basic existential position and that person's development of a life script. People have a characteristic way of looking at and experiencing themselves and other people. This characteristic way is the *existential position*. There are four basic positions: (1) "I'm OK: You're OK"—the healthy position. (2) "I'm OK: You're not OK"—the mistrustful position. (3) "I'm not OK: You're OK"—the dependent and depressed position. (4) "I'm not OK: You're not OK"—the unhealthy position. What is important to note about these positions is that they tend to influence the nature and quality of all human interactions. For example, a person who does not feel good about himself becomes more comfortable with negative strokes than with positive strokes. More often than not he refuses positive strokes, seeing himself as undeserving of them. Such a person goes out of his way to collect negative strokes. In another example, a person who feels good about himself but not about others becomes suspicious and uncaring. He tends to view others as irresponsible, untrustworthy, and unworthy. More often than not he seeks to control others and use them to get strokes of which he is ultimately suspicious and which he discounts, since the givers really do not count. Other people are merely objects to manipulate for his own ends.

On the basis of existential positions, people construct systems of interaction and write life scripts that they play out in all interactions with others. All scripts fall under one of three types: *winning scripts*, *losing scripts*, or *banal scripts*. Winning scripts allow joy, fulfillment, growth, and quality relations. Losing scripts allow hurt, unfulfillment, regression, and stressful relations. Banal scripts allow emptiness, boredom, tedium, and isolation. Since scripts are written quite early in life, a clue can be found in determining a person's favorite childhood story. The plot, main character, and the climax of such a story point to the type of script a person is living.

The complexities and vagaries of this model are beyond the scope of this book. The reader may wish to refer to Berne's two books for a detailed presentation. Some mention of the "games people play" should be made, however, before leaving this model. A *game* is defined as a series of transactions that structures time and protects people from intimacy. By filling time and deflecting people from the richness and risks involved in intimacy, games only lead to an appearance of stability and mutuality in any relationship. By precluding open and direct interaction, they ultimately lead to overwhelmingly bad feelings, to needs being unmet, and to the dissolution of a relationship.

In any interaction words, nonverbal cues, and interpersonal styles are in part determined by ego states, existential positions, strokes, scripts, and particularly by that peculiar form of transaction, games. Regardless of the apparent simplicity in an interaction and regardless of the overt content of an interaction, contact between two or more people involves elements described by this model. If nothing else, transactional analysis provides a structure by which anyone can analyze past interactions, understand transactional events as they unfold in the present, and predict at least his own contributions to future interactions.

It has been the authors' experience that not infrequently what start out as relatively simple interactions quickly take on emotional tones and surplus meanings over and above what was intended by either party. It has also been their experience that reframing such events, using transactional analysis or any other of a number of models described in this book, has put these events in a clearer perspective. More important, the reframing has helped them deal more effectively with other, similar situations. The reader is asked, therefore, to return to the opening scene of this chapter. What ego states appeared to be in operation both in the young woman and in Leslie? What might Leslie's offer to talk have connoted to the young woman? What might Leslie have done differently to help?

Effectiveness Training

At the base of effectiveness training is the notion of *problem ownership* and the skills of *active listening* and giving *I-messages*. Gordon, in three books (1970, 1974, 1977), detailed this model for parents, teachers, and managers. The model will be summarized here and related to library service.

All individuals who work with other people view them through a filter. Certain behaviors exhibited by others are acceptable, while others are unacceptable. All of these behaviors fall within what Gordon calls the "behavior rectangle." Everything another person might say or do is contained within that rectangle. A filter divides the rectangle into two areas, the *area of acceptance* and the *area of nonacceptance*. Figure 3 shows a sample rectangle with sample behaviors.

The filter-line does not remain fixed. Three factors cause it to move up or down. These are: (1) changes in self; (2) changes in the other

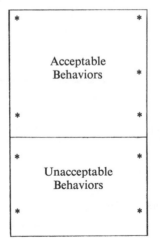

Person works quietly in the reference room.	*		*	Person quietly uses card catalog.
		Acceptable Behaviors	*	Person returns materials to their appropriate place.
Person helps another find materials.	*		*	Person follows your instructions.
Person interrupts while you are instructing another.	*	Unacceptable Behaviors	*	Person does not return materials to appropriate place.
Person tears articles out of a journal.	*		*	Person makes noise in the reading room.

Figure 3.   Library Behaviors, the Areas of Acceptance and Nonacceptance, and the Behavior Rectangle

person; and (3) changes in the situation or the environment. The first includes, for example, fatigue, a good day, a bad day, feeling ill, just having received a reprimand by a supervisor, and so forth. The second includes such items as physical appearance, past history with the person, the other's mood, and so forth. The third includes the reading room, the check-out desk, a book sale in the main lobby, and so forth.

Refining the rectangle and the acceptable-unacceptable distinction further leads to the notion of problem-ownership. By and large, things that a person does or says are acceptable if they do not interfere with a librarian meeting his needs, doing his job. Things that a person does or says are unacceptable if they do interfere with the librarian meeting his needs, doing his job. When things interfere, the librarian owns the problem. For example, when another person tears pages out of a journal, causing the librarian time and effort to deal with this and money to replace the journal, the librarian owns that problem. Or, when a person reveals to the librarian anger and disappointment because his spouse will not allow him to work as a volunteer in the children's room, this in no way tangibly or concretely affects the librarian (assuming that the librarian will not have to work extra hours because of this). The other person owns the problem. In the first example the behavior falls below the filter-line—unacceptable behavior that causes a problem for the librarian. In the second example the behavior falls above the filter-line—acceptable behavior that does not cause a problem with the librarian. In this second case, the other has the problem. These two examples are represented in figure 4.

There are times when another person says or does things that neither cause the librarian a problem nor show that the person has a problem. When this happens there is *no problem* in the relationship. For example, a person might help another learn the skills for using a microfilm reader or for using the card catalog. This example is represented in figure 5.

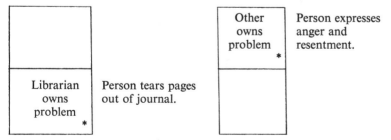

Figure 4.   Examples of Problem Ownership Seen through the Behavior Rectangle

Other owns problem
No Problem *
Librarian owns problem

One person helps another with a piece of library equipment.

Figure 5.   An Example of "No Problem" Behavior

This no-problem area is where work goes on, where teaching and learning occur, where relationships carry on.

The difference between other-owned and librarian-owned problems is essentially one of tangible and concrete effect. The librarian, then, might do well to ask the following questions when confronted by problematic behaviors. Does this behavior have any real, tangible, or concrete effect on me? Am I feeling unaccepting because I am being interfered with, damaged, hurt, impaired in some way? Or am I feeling unaccepting merely because I would like the other person to act differently or to not have a problem? If the answer is yes to the first two questions, the problem belongs to the librarian. If the answer is yes to the third question, the problem belongs to the other.

What can an individual do if another person has a problem? Helping is a skill. Many of the things people say or do under the guise of helping are really not helpful at all. Gordon called these typical, unhelpful attempts at helping "the dirty dozen." These do not indicate to the person with the problem that he is being heard, understood, or accepted. Here, then, are "the dirty dozen": (1) ordering, commanding, directing; (2) warning, threatening; (3) moralizing, preaching, giving "shoulds" and "oughts"; (4) advising, offering solutions or suggestions; (5) teaching, lecturing, giving logical arguments; (6) judging, criticizing, disagreeing, blaming; (7) name-calling, stereotyping, labeling; (8) interpreting, analyzing, diagnosing; (9) praising, agreeing, giving positive evaluations; (10) reassuring, sympathizing, consoling, supporting; (11) questioning, probing, interrogating, cross-examining; and (12) withdrawing, distracting, being sarcastic, humoring, diverting.

"The dirty dozen" do not help. Instead they communicate unacceptance, judgment, denial of the problem as real, avoidance, or superiority. To highlight this, the authors would like the reader to perform an experiment. Using the situation listed above, in which a person has expressed anger and disappointment about not being able to volunteer in the library, write twelve typical helping statements, one for each of the "dirty dozen." Next, tally those that you in fact used in similar situations with people who have problems; also tally those personally experienced when you expressed a problem to another. Are you helpful when you use the twelve? Have you been helped when the twelve were used on you?

Truly helping statements or behaviors indicate to the person with the problem that he is being heard, understood, and accepted. These are: (1) passive listening—a powerful nonverbal message of acceptance; (2) acknowledgment responses—nodding, leaning forward, smiling, and the now classic verbal cues "uh-huh," "oh," "I see"; (3) dooropeners—encouraging verbal statements such as "would you like to say more about that?" or, "sounds like you have some strong feelings about that"; and (4) active listening—paraphrasing the words and reflecting the underlying feelings in a statement. These helping responses are all open-ended. They in no way contain or communicate evaluation of what is being said. They indicate understanding of what is being said. They all communicate acceptance and trust. Active listening is the most powerful of the helping responses. Below are three dialogues between a librarian and another person that exemplify this skill.

DIALOGUE NO. 1

Student: Bill just checked out a book I need.

Librarian: That's right, he did.

Student: Yeah. Now I won't be able to finish the assignment for Mr. Bowen.

Librarian: You're worried about that?

Student: It's an important one. And now I won't get a good grade.

Librarian: Oh! You're concerned about the grade.

Student: My mother and father won't like it if I don't get a good grade.

Librarian: They won't? You're really worried about what your mother and father will feel?

Student: Yeah. They sure want me to get a good grade. Now what'll I do?

Librarian: You're not sure of how to get the assignment done?

Student: Not really.

Librarian: This assignment means a lot to you?

Student: Sure. What'll I do?

Librarian: Would you like some help?

Student: Would you help?

Librarian: Yes. What's the topic? Maybe we can find some other materials you could use.

DIALOGUE NO. 2

Student-Librarian: Damn, damn, damn!

Librarian: Wow! You're really upset.

Student-Librarian: Here it is the end of the semester. I hadn't seen Professor Carter all semester. He comes in here yesterday, observes me for an hour, and gives me a lousy evaluation.

Librarian: It sounds like you're worried about that evaluation and you're angry at Carter.

Student-Librarian: Yes! If this is graduate school. . . . What a mess!

Librarian: You're worried about how that evaluation will affect your chances of getting a job.

Student-Librarian: (Dejectedly) Yeah. He's a pretty big name in the field. I don't know what to do.

Librarian: You seem really dejected.

Student-Librarian: I am!

Librarian: Who else do you think evaluates you?

Student-Librarian: I don't know. . . .

Librarian: Think about it.

Student-Librarian: (Cautiously) Oh, I suppose someone here does.

Librarian: Yes, I do.

Student-Librarian: You do?

Librarian: Yes. Come on—you must remember that the procedure was explained at the beginning of the semester.

Student-Librarian: (Hesitantly) Well, I guess I do.

Librarian: Betsy, I've worked with you all semester and I've really liked what I've seen. Now I know that this isn't the time or place to go over your evaluation. And I know that Professor Carter's means a lot to you. But I think you have done a good job.

Student-Librarian: Do you?

Librarian: Yes! Maybe we'd better set a time so that I can go over your evaluation with you. How about it?

Student-Librarian: O.K. Sure.

Librarian: I didn't mean to not listen to your feelings about Carter. But I thought you should know generally how I saw your work.

Student-Librarian: Thanks. I understand.

Librarian: Good, you're welcome. How about 9:00 A.M. tomorrow for our meeting?

Student-Librarian: (Cheerfully) Fine.

DIALOGUE NO. 3

Librarian: You look so overwrought.

Person: What of it!

Librarian: You seem angry for some reason.

Person: Leave me alone!

Librarian: Would you like to talk about it?

Person: What do you care!

Librarian: You're not sure whether you can trust me.

Person: Why should I?

Librarian: You're not sure about whether I can help.

Person: You can't!

Librarian: I see.

Person: Nobody can. I've just come from the vet's where my dog was put to sleep. He got hit by a car. I only came in here because this has always been a peaceful place.

Librarian: You're really sad about losing your dog.

Person: That's not all. I went to get a cup of coffee. And when I came back, my case was gone.

Librarian: Oh! You're upset and frustrated about having your case stolen.

Person: Yeah! And do you know why?

Librarian: Do you want to tell me?

Person: The only picture I had of Bruno was in that case. Now he's gone and I don't even have the picture to remind me of him.

Librarian: Oh!

Person: What kind of place are you running here, a library or a thief's training ground?

Librarian: You think the library's responsible for your loss.

Person: No . . . not really. I guess I'm just getting old and forgetful.

Librarian: You're sad.

Person: Yes. But you know, I've lost a lot of friends and I survived . . . Why just yesterday I was thinking that Bruno was getting pretty old and lame. I even was considering putting him to sleep. And maybe even buying a new puppy.

Librarian: You were anticipating losing an old friend.

Person: Yeah, I was. Well, I do feel somewhat better. And after all, I did come here to borrow some books. Thanks.

Librarian: You're welcome.

Active listening sometimes merely allows the person to get the problem off his chest. Sometimes it allows the person to clarify the problem and to solve it himself. At other times, the helper jointly solves the problem with the person. And at still other times, the problem does not get solved.

What about situations in which the librarian owns the problem?

When another person is causing a problem, he and the behavior must be confronted. Typically, such confrontation takes several forms. First, the librarian might use a *solution message*. "If you do not stop tearing out journal pages, you will be forbidden to come into this building again!" In such a case the librarian is handing out the solution to his own problem and expecting that the person will buy it. Second, he might use a *put-down message*. "You are a destructive pest for tearing out those pages!" In this case the librarian did little but ridicule the person. The problem has hardly been solved. Third, the librarian might try an *indirect message*. "I understand that they are looking for paper-shredders at Scott Paper Company!" Here, in addition to communicating sarcasm, the message may not even be understood. Finally, the librarian might try a *you-message*. "You ought to know better than to do such a thing!" or "You're not behaving like a mature person!" or "You stop that!" Any of "the dirty dozen" can be used to construct a you-message. In these cases, the librarian is laying blame and not owning responsibility for his own feelings.

The effective alternative is the *I-message*. Another name given to this type of message is the "responsibility-message." The librarian who sends such a message is taking responsibility for his own feelings by sharing these and leaving responsibility for the other's behavior with the other. An I-message has three components: (1) a description of the feeling; (2) a description of the behavior in question, and (3) a statement of the tangible, concrete effect on the sender. Returning to the example, the librarian could say, "I get extremely upset when you tear pages out of journals because I have to spend time reordering them and finding temporary replacements" or "When I see you tearing out pages, I get very frustrated and angry because I have to replace them and that takes time and money!"

At this point the authors would like the reader to perform another experiment. Think about a recent situation in which a person was doing something unacceptable, causing some interference, and creating a problem. What did you do? What did you say? Consider the situation and develop an I-message. Make a commitment to use several I-messages when situations that cause you problems occur in the future.

Gordon approaches problem solving in as nonjudgmental a way as possible. He allows both parties to take responsibility for their behaviors and for their feelings. He is nonjudgmental, allows cooperation, and both parties experience "no-lose" solutions to problems no matter who owns them.

To complete this section, the authors again ask the reader to think back on the opening scene of this chapter and answer the following questions. Who owned the problem as presented? What did Leslie do? What might she have done differently to be helpful? What type of statement or message might have reached the young woman? Have you ever found yourself in similar situations?

Reality Therapy

Several key assumptions underlie Glasser's (1965) model. First, people chose the ways in which they live. Second, people who experience recurrent difficulties in living deny their choices or indicate that the available choices are either not appropriate or not good for them. Third, there are very few optionless situations.

For Glasser, humans operate on a continuum ranging from extreme failure to success. They start from the "security position" and choose to move toward success or failure. There are four regular "success pathways." These are: (1) giving and receiving love; (2) gaining worth and recognition; (3) having fun; and (4) becoming self-disciplined These pathways lead to a "success identity." This is characterized by any person doing things in his life that he wants to do, that enhance his self-concept, that neither harm him nor others around him. Opportunities to succeed lead a person to strength and self-confidence. Success in such opportunities is dependent on a person's ability to make a plan and his willingness to follow through with it in a responsible and self-disciplined manner. When a person does not experience opportunities and does not experience strength, he feels pain. In an attempt to reduce this pain he gives up choices or responsibilities; consequently he moves toward failure. A "failure identity" is characterized by the inability to cope, by wariness and by the general belief that change is impossible.

The move toward failure temporarily reduces pain. The pain, however, does return. In another attempt to reduce pain, the person denies his failure and chooses symptoms. Glasser classified symptoms into four types: (1) acting-out; (2) emotional upset; (3) psychotic manifestations; and (4) psychosomatic representations. Thus for Glasser a symptom, whatever one a person chooses, is a denial of failure, inadequacies, or irresponsibility. Symptoms do not work well for any extended periods of time. Eventually the pain returns with the added burden of the misery the symptoms bring with them. In a new attempt to escape the pain and find pleasure in failure, the person chooses an addiction (e.g., food, alcohol, drugs, and so forth). For the addict everything goes but his addiction. He chooses only it.

Before continuing, any objections forming in the reader's mind must be dispelled. As a librarian, one might come across failure-types—but symptom-types, addict-types? The authors refer the reader to Carol Easton's article, "Sex and Violence in the Library: Scream a Little Louder, Please" (1977) for a clearly reported picture of the "types" librarians meet in big city public libraries. Since deviance is not restricted to big cities and since rural crime and rural mental health problems need not take second place to their urban counterparts, read on. Remember, however, that the authors do not argue here for librarians to assume a therapeutic role. The skills described here are useful in helping the librarian in disengaging from the troubled person and working on less extreme, less difficult problems.

For Glasser, "therapy" is the attempt to help a person be responsible for his choices and to assist that person in making plans to choose, change, and move toward success. Therapy need not be done only by professionals. The helping role can be played by anyone willing to commit himself to another human being. The steps in a helping process are as follows: (1) Make friends. Those who need help are lonely. Give a little of yourself (i.e., your time, your interests, your beliefs, your humor, and so forth); it is strengthening. (2) Emphasize present behavior. Repeatedly ask this question, "What are you doing now?" Be specific and help the other person focus on actual behavior. (3) Help the person determine whether his present behavior is helpful or nonhelpful, good or bad, functional or dysfunctional. Is the behavior something the person wants to choose to do in the long run, in the future? This step requires that the person make a clear and direct *value judgment* regarding his behavior. (4) Help the person develop a plan to do something different, something better, something good, something helpful. Choosing different behavior opens the door to the four regular success pathways. Insure that the plan is specific and simple enough to insure some success. (5) Obtain a commitment to the plan. Focus on the when, where, how, and so forth. Set a time to review the plan, the changes, and the new choices. (6) Do not ask for, get involved with, or accept excuses. Excuses are clues to the ways in which the person will maintain his failure. (7) Do not punish when the plan does not work. All that matters is that there are consequences (i.e., natural and/or logical social consequences) to the old and the new behavior. (8) Do not give up. "Hang in" with the person beyond the point at which others have given up and beyond the point at which he predicts you will give up.

The eight steps are circular. When and if you reach number eight, you are back at number one. For Glasser, therapy is the giving of self, strength, and affection. He strongly emphasized this and stressed that without involvement at such a level, hard-nosed failures will continue to fail.

To close this section, the authors again ask the reader to think back on the opening scene of this chapter. How might Leslie have become involved with the young woman? What might Leslie have done to give of herself? How could Leslie have kept the young woman with her long enough to learn more about what was troubling her?

The three models are powerful. They clearly obtain results. Yet they have several weaknesses. The language of transactional analysis smacks of jargon. In an attempt to describe and explain the structure of the human personality, writers in transactional analysis have added more and more concepts and more and more words to their model. Some of these words were evident above. Closely associated with the language problem and perhaps even causing it is the complexity of the model. Not satisfied with simply structuring the human personality into Parent, Adult and Child, writers have restructured it several times. Second and third-order structural analyses make an already complex model unnecessarily complex. Another example of this is the theoretical position of scripts, counter-scripts, and episcripts. From the perspective of this book the increasing level of complexity is unnecessary.

Transactional analysts tend toward exclusivity. They represent a closed club, not only in their view of an approach to helping, but also in their formal and formalistic training programs. Indeed, they make it hard for most people to practice transactional analysis.

Transactional analysis is a theoretical model. It does not provide many practical communication skills. Likewise it suffers the same fate of most awareness models; that is, awareness does not necessarily lead to change.

Perhaps the greatest problem results in response to the weaknesses noted above. That is, people have a tendency to oversimplify transactional analysis. For an example of this the reader is referred to J. P. Wilkinson's article "The Psycho-Organizational Approach to Staff Communication in Libraries" (1978).

Effectiveness training is prone to the "true believer" syndrome. People who practice it tend to do so to the exclusion of other models. The model clearly overlooks other ways to help and other ways to share deep feelings. Thus, seeing effectiveness training as the "one true way" is understandable. Its language is relatively simple, and so the model is prone to oversimplification, repetitiveness, and boredom. Moreover, the language is easy to read, easy to predict, and easy to manipulate. Often the skills are abused in order to allow a person to avoid responsibility. The phrase "It's your problem" is often used to assist in this avoidance. Effectiveness training may lead to better feelings but often not to problem solving.

Reality therapy's greatest strength is also perhaps its greatest weakness. That is, the model requires involvement. At times involving oneself with people with problems is difficult. Reality therapy is also prone to the "true believer" syndrome. People who practice reality therapy use it exclusively. The model requires a high degree of skill even though it appears simple initially. This causes another weakness—the misuse of the model by novices and people who misread and use it in a punitive way. In the latter case, people will use discipline and the notion of "no excuses" as punishment. A number of children exposed to reality therapy in public schools comment on the ease with which they can manipulate both model and practitioners to get attention and avoid taking charge of their lives. Finally, reality therapy tends to overlook such external forces as family and peer pressures that cause difficulties, while viewing all problems through the "colored glasses" of responsibility-irresponsibility.

The Library and Helping

A number of situations confront modern-day librarians. The young woman in the opening scene, people with failure identities—are these people experiencing problems beyond the ken and experience of librarians? Perhaps. Yet the authors' experiences as a psychologist and a librarian indicate that the library often becomes a focal point for troubled people. In a number of schools known to the authors, teachers often use the library as a "time-out" facility. That is, they send individuals, small groups of students, or entire classes to the library when either the student(s) or the teacher needs a break, time away from the regular class structure and from each other. This particularly happens with students who are explosive, intrusive, and uncontrollable. In more than one school the library is used as an in-school detention center. In others the library serves as a haven for students who wish to temporarily avoid or entirely escape the repetitiveness, tedium, and frustration of the classroom. Many in-school dropouts regularly use the library as a sanctuary, a last resort against their failure syndrome. Even in the authors' small Maine town the local library provides a meeting place for lonely elderly people, transients, the disenchanted, and other types. Redl (1966) even documents the therapeutic use of the library for hyperaggressive children. So perhaps the library and librarians have been quietly placed in a new role, a role that makes these three models and this book more important.

At first glance the demands of this new bibliotherapeutic role seem overwhelming. No case is being made here for turning libraries into alternative therapeutic communities. The realization must be faced, however, that libraries are facing changes in their function. The troublesome and the troubled are not excluded from libraries by virtue of their problems and, since they come into libraries, they need to be worked with and helped.

The key points of the models are important. At first they appear to be related only because they are designed to make sense out of people problems; their differences seem more obvious. Yet they have one important commonality: they reformulate or reframe problems. Transactional analysis views and restructures interaction. It points out that interpersonal difficulties arise out of premature decisions. Since this is so, redecisions can be made to change both the circumstances and the problematic interchanges. Effectiveness training redescribes and relocates problems in terms of problem ownership. This and this alone could cause behavior to change, but there is more. The helping behaviors offered by this model reframe and clarify problems. The model thus offers considerable relief and freedom through the realization that a behavior or a circumstance is not a person's problem and that the reframed problem is not so overwhelming. Thus, energy is freed up to work in different ways toward solutions. Reality therapy relabels problems as outward manifestations of irresponsibility. Specifically, a symptom arises out of a person's unwillingness to deal responsibly and effectively with the situation, rather than ineffectuality arising out of the symptom. For example, this model holds that people are depressed because they are doing nothing, rather than that people are unable to do things because of depression.

The reformulation or reframing of problems was addressed directly by Haley (1963) and by Watzlawick, Weakland, and Fisch (1974). Working within the context of communication and the theory of circular systems, Haley and Watzlawick argued that human relations in general and symptomatic behavior in particular reflect the ongoing tactical struggle for predictability, for control of relationships and of events.

This position requires a closer look. In addition to the verbal messages that people communicate, they also communicate about the communication with nonverbal cues that either support or contradict their verbal messages. These qualifiers include other verbal messages, nonverbal cues, and the context in which communication takes place. Several rules apply in human communicative relations. First, one cannot fail to qualify a message. There is always a message about the message. Qualification can be either congruent (i.e., affirming the message) or incongruent (i.e., negating the message). Second, as one cannot fail to qualify a message, one cannot fail to indicate the behavior to take place in the relationship; that is, qualifiers indicate who is to control the types of messages and the definition of the relationship. Third, one cannot avoid being in a struggle over the definition of his relationship with someone else. A simple example highlights these rules. A man and woman meet for the first time. Initially they exchange a number of verbal messages. Soon, however, the man gingerly puts his arm around the woman. This nonverbal gesture is an attempt to define the relationship as a romantic or physical one, an attempt to indicate the behaviors to take place and to establish control in the relationship. Now the woman responds. Verbally she states, "No, no." She has a choice regarding how she qualifies her message. She can move away, in which case she qualifies it congruently with her nonverbal message. Or she can move slightly closer to the man (or not move at all), in which case she qualifies her message incongruently in the same fashion. Whichever she chooses to do, she will counter the man's attempt to define and control the relationship with her own attempt. These moves and countermoves are maneuvers, messages that place the relationship in question.

Watzlawick, Beavin, and Jackson (1967) presented three types of communicative relationships. In a *symmetrical* relationship people communicate as equals. In a *complementary* relationship people communicate as unequals, as in the typical superior-subordinate relationship. In a *metacomplementary* relationship one person lets or forces the other to define the relationship and its behaviors in a certain way. This last type of relationship is important for several reasons. First its subtlety and indirectness make the complexities of a relationship even more complicated. Second, it makes communication more difficult. Third, whoever establishes the metacomplementary relationship is, in fact, defining and controlling the nature and degree of behaviors involved in that relationship. Fourth, this type of relationship involves a paradox (i.e., I am telling you what to tell me to do) that can lead to confusion and to a denial (by the establisher) of attempts to gain and to maintain control.

One particular relationship brings the issue of metacomplementarity into bold relief—the helping relationship. Haley argued that problems as symptoms are metacomplementary tactics for control of a relationship. Moreover, he emphasized that problem solving is best carried out by posing paradoxes that reverse metacomplementary tactics used by the person seeking help. For example, an insomniac's sleeplessness interferes with his other tasks and functions. The more he wants to sleep, the more he tries to sleep, the less he sleeps. The single most effective way to solve the problem posed by insomnia is to encourage a paradox—that the person remain awake. Not knowing this, the person comes seeking help. The helper indicates that change can take place. Within this change-framework, the helper permits and encourages the person to continue with the behavior. In fact he encourages and even engineers the situation so that the insomniac stays awake. The helper has posed a paradox of his own. His directive to stay awake, coupled with his indication that the person can change his sleeplessness, represent both an incongruence and a reframing. When the insomniac is offered two directives (i.e., stay awake and go to sleep) that conflict with each other and that demand a response, he can respond by indicating that he is not responding to either directive. Paradoxically, he succeeds spontaneously at falling asleep.

Problems and problem solving in communications, then, are matters of paradox (Haley, 1963; Watzlawick et al., 1967; Watzlawick et al., 1974). To summarize, a person with a problem behaves in a certain extreme way while denying that he is in control of such behavior. The helper directs the person, simultaneously indicating that the other should not follow his directives. The other person then responds, indicating that he is not responding to the directives of the helper, but rather that he is responding spontaneously and behaving differently. The helper's role is to reframe the problem and by so doing allow alternatives to be experienced spontaneously. This framing/reframing sequence is part and parcel of transactional analysis, effectiveness training, and reality therapy. All three work with difficult problems. All three allow a reframing of the problem; the awareness of one's script and a redecision (transactional analysis); the location of a problem and the different styles of dealing with it (effectiveness training); the value judgment and the change-plan for unchangeable behavior (reality therapy). The case study below, using a reality therapy format, will highlight and recap this concept. The reader will have an opportunity to practice reframing with this chapter's learning exercise.

Karen: A Case Study

Karen was a ninth-grade student at a rural regional high school. She never managed to go to class for more than a few days each grading period. Her past records showed that this pattern had occurred for at least two years. Her sole preoccupation in school was to seek out teachers and other adults to talk about "how awful" everything was. Her home life was stable, uneventful, but with little or no interest, involvement, or affection expressed by or with her parents. She was in danger of failing most if not all of her courses.

The guidance counselors had attempted everything in their kit-bag to involve Karen and help her find some success in school. All attempts had failed. A series of team meetings had led to little but frustration for all concerned. Karen was not happy, but her behavior was considered "all right" in her opinion. As a last resort, a consulting psychologist was asked to see her. Reviewing her records, he noted that she had been evaluated numberless times in the past. All these evaluations pointed to a girl of average intelligence with no motivation for school work. No major psychological problems were reported.

The psychologist devoted his first three sessions with Karen to finding out what she liked to do—apparently very little. She had no interests, no close friends, and no commitments. She made contact with the people and the objects in her world only in a peripheral way. The only positive aspect of his contact was discovering that she felt powerless to affect her life or those around her and she felt badly about this situation. It was, at least, a starting point. As he culled what little he could from his notes in preparation for a fourth and final session, he recalled that on the past three occasions he had found Karen not in her scheduled classes but in the media center talking quite cordially and animatedly with the head librarian. A quick phone call revealed that Karen spent most of her time in the media center. Before the fourth session he met with the librarian and obtained a commitment from her to work with Karen in some way. In the fourth session, the psychologist casually mentioned the library. This set off a long declaration from Karen about how nice the media center was and how friendly the librarians were. The psychologist carefully observed that the library seemed Karen's only positive interest in school; she acknowledged this. He indicated that perhaps she might spend more time there. Karen gave him a perplexed look. Not quite asking why, she commented on whether or not her other teachers would approve. The psychologist assured her that they would not object. Karen indicated that it would be "nice." She quickly stated that while spending time there she could never bring herself to do any schoolwork. The psychologist responded by answering her that "that would not be expected." Karen agreed.

They then met with the media center staff. All agreed that the plan was acceptable if Karen would assist them in their day-to-day activities. Karen agreed to this. Each week the psychologist checked in with the library staff. After four weeks things were going well; Karen assisted in filing catalog cards, finding materials, working with the library study groups, recording new acquisitions, and giving book-talks in a variety of classes. The only problem seemed to be Karen's growing enthusiasm. She not only spent the school day there, but also spent long hours in the late afternoon and the evening. Both of these times were slow periods and Karen had little to do. The psychologist decided to check back with her.

Late one evening he wandered into the media center to find Karen engrossed in a history book. When she saw the psychologist she was quick to claim, "Oh hi; I wasn't reading this for school!" He accepted the statement and allowed that that was good, since that was not "what was expected of her." They talked for a while, mostly about the book. Karen proudly showed him a notebook in which she was recording her thoughts and impressions about history. After a bit of inner turmoil the psychologist suggested several novels that related to the period about which she was reading. She replied that she would perhaps find them tomorrow. She quickly claimed, however, that she was not doing so as schoolwork. He agreed.

The next week Karen sought out the psychologist to tell him how much she enjoyed one of the recommended books. She also showed him an essay she had written on it. Not only was this essay the first complete piece of written work that Karen had done in three years, but it was also very well done. The psychologist commented on the essay. Karen seemed happy and proud. In discussion of this serendipitous event with the library staff, one suggested that Karen might read the essay as part of a classroom discussion of historical fiction. The only possible difficulty was that the class in which the discussion was to take place was one in which Karen had experienced more than a modicum of conflict. Rather than suggest a situation that would entail any possible chance of failure, it was suggested that she read it in the library during book week. The psychologist suggested this to Karen and she agreed.

The reading went well and Karen presented herself in a way that few had ever seen. She appeared poised and mature. Of more importance, she seemed satisfied with her success. It was not long after this reading that she asked to see the psychologist. She indicated that she was becoming interested in two classes offered in the spring quarter, European History and Literature of Europe. The psychologist asked what she might do to arrange going to these classes. She was unsure. He then asked if she would be willing to think about a plan to reenter the two classes and work on it with him. She said yes, "and after all I do get bored spending all my time in the library!"

Planning took about three weeks. The plan included a letter from Karen to the two teachers requesting admission, a sit down session with the teachers concerning expected and acceptable behavior, and a biweekly conference with the psychologist, the teachers, and Karen to discuss process and progress. In addition, Karen planned to continue her work in the library. This was agreed upon by all concerned.

Now, one year later, Karen has just reentered her final class. She is taking a full sophomore course load. And she continues her work in the library, only now for a small salary. A success? Maybe. Only time will tell.

AN EXERCISE

Changing: A Structured Process

This procedure is a modification of Weinstein's Trumpet Processing Guide (Weinstein, 1973). It provides an excellent way to reframe problems. Select a recent problem, but one that you see recurring, and apply the process.

THE PROCESS

A. Confronting and inventorying responses
   1. What happened? What did you do? What specific actions did you take?
   2. At which point did you feel most comfortable? Most uncomfortable? Describe any of the feelings that you had.
   3. What did you say to yourself? What did you tell yourself to do?
   4. How many of the things you told yourself involved "shoulds or should nots"? What were they?
B. Recognizing and clarifying patterns
   1. How was your response typical of you?
   2. In what kinds of situations do you usually respond that way? When, where, and under what conditions?
   3. What would be the exact opposite response from yours? Describe it in detail.
   4. Fill in the following: "Whenever I'm in a situation where ———, I usually experience feelings of ———. I tell myself ———, and what I do is ———."
C. Owning patterns by clarifying function
   1. What does your pattern (your typical response) do for you?
   2. What does your pattern get for you, either from others or from yourself?
   3. What does your pattern help you avoid?
   4. What feelings does your pattern protect you from?
D. Consequences
   1. Is your pattern getting you what you want?
   2. Are there some effects of your pattern that you *do not* like?
   3. What price are you paying for your pattern?
   4. Are you missing out on anything by responding this way? What?

E. Alternatives
  1. Imagine the "perfect solution." This solution does not cost you as much as your original pattern. Picture yourself with this solution, with this new set of responses, in:
     a. A situation at work
     b. A circumstance at home
     c. A social occasion (one appropriate to person and pattern).
  2. Answer the following:
     a. What new behaviors would you be showing?
     b. What differences in you would colleagues, relatives, and friends see? What would they say?
     c. What new feelings would you have about yourself?
     d. How would these new feelings affect you?
  3. Decide on several situations in which you will try out or experiment with the solution.
  4. Pick one or two that will come up in the near future.
     a. What inside you will attempt to sabotage the solution?
     b. What inside you will allow you to succeed?
  5. Involve another person in your solution and its specifics. Decide on how and when you will report progress to this person.
F. Evaluation
  1. What happened to the experiment with the solution?
  2. What were some of the thoughts, feelings, and consequences that resulted?
  3. Did the solution seem adequate? Does it need any revisions?
  4. What else might you try?
G. Choice
  1. What decisions are you ready to make about your pattern and alternative behaviors?
  2. Fill in the following: "Whenever I ———— (confrontation), I anticipate that ———— (thought). So I usually ———— (feelings, behaviors, typical reaction). I react that way in order to get and/or avoid ———— (function). But in the process, ———— (consequences, price paid). So what I really prefer is ———— (an ideal end-state). The next time I found myself in that situation, I tried the following experiments:
     a. ————————————————————————————————————.
     b. ————————————————————————————————————.
     c. ————————————————————————————————————.
     I liked what happened when I tried ———— (specific experiment), so from now on I am going to ———— (choice)."

The procedure certainly ties in both Glasser's notions about describing and evaluating behaviors and some transactional analysis concepts. Thus the process can be supplemented by more from both of these models. The process works with individuals and in a group setting, in which pairs or trios work as support subgroups.

References

Anderson, John P. *A transactional analysis primer.* In J. Jones and J. W. Pfeiffer (eds.), *The 1973 Annual Handbook for Group Facilitators.* La Jolla, Calif.: University Associates, 1973.

Berne, Eric. *Games people play.* New York: Grove Press, 1964.

———. *Transactional analysis in psychotherapy.* New York: Grove Press, 1961.

Easton, Carol. Sex and violence in the library: Scream a little louder, please. *American Libraries,* 1977, *8,* 484–88.

Glasser, William. *Reality therapy.* New York: Harper & Row, 1965.

Gordon, Thomas. *Leader effectiveness training.* New York: Wyden, 1977.

———. *Parent effectiveness training.* New York: Wyden, 1970.

———. *Teacher effectiveness training.* New York: Wyden, 1974.

Haley, Jay. *Strategies of psychotherapy.* New York: Grune & Stratton, 1963.

Redl, Fritz. The furious children in the library. In F. Redl (ed.), *When we deal with children.* New York: Free Press, 1966.

Watzlawick, Paul, Beavin, Janet, and Jackson, Don. *Pragmatics of human communication.* New York: Norton, 1967.

———, Weakland, John, and Fisch, Richard. *Change: Principles of problem formation and problem resolution.* New York: Norton, 1974.

Weinstein, Gerald. Self-science education: The trumpet. *Personnel and Guidance Journal,* 1973, *5,* 600-6.

Wilkinson, J. P. The psycho-organizational approach to staff communication in libraries. *The Journal of Academic Librarianship,* 1978, *4,* 21–26.

8 Groupwork

The Wonderful World of 301.18

The Scene: Evening at a high school library/media center. Two groups of between 40 and 50 people each are gathered together in the library's art gallery for a meeting called by the head librarian. One group consists of adults who have classes at the high school in the evening and a few of their teachers. The other group consists of high school day students who regularly use the library in the evening. There is visible tension between the two groups.

At the appointed time for the meeting to begin, the librarian asks that the adult students and their teachers form a circle in the center of the room. She then asks the high school students to sit in a circle around the adults. (This is called a fishbowl discussion technique.) She instructs the adults to describe and discuss their impressions of what seems to be a serious problem between the day students and those who go to school in the evening. She explains that each person who desires will be given an opportunity to speak briefly, and that she will act as moderator to make sure that the 20 minutes allotted for discussion are fairly shared. She tells the day students that they will have their 20 minutes next. She asks that they refrain from comments or questions during the adults' speaking time, and that the adults do the same when the young peoples' turn arrives. She asks that each group listen carefully to what the other has to say.

The adult discussion begins when one elderly man states that he is a taxpayer in this community, as well as a student, and that as such he has a right to use the library without a bunch of kids hassling him. A woman speaks next, saying that she has never seen such rude youngsters in her life. "All I want to do is study quietly, and there they are talking, laughing, and making rude noises. Why can't they go elsewhere to fool around? Why do they have to be here? They have the daytime. Isn't that enough? Isn't the library supposed to be for quiet reading and studying? In my day it was." An adult education faculty member then speaks up. "I'm embarrassed to bring my classes here. They are subject to abusive language and made fun of if they happen to look the least bit different from these kids. It's gotten so my students don't dare to set foot in here. I want them to enjoy using the library, not to be afraid of it. This kind of thing has got to stop!"

The day students are obviously angry at what they are hearing, but abide by the guidelines given for discussion and wait their turn. When the librarian determines that all adults have said what they need to say, she then asks the day students to follow the same procedure. The inner and outer groups change places.

A student who has barely contained himself throughout the adult's discussion now speaks out. "This building is for us. This is the high school, and this library is ours. You people have had your chance at an education. Now it is our turn. Why don't you go home, relax, and watch television?"

Another student nods her head vigorously in agreement and adds, "You ought to use the public library. You could go there instead." Then one of the others says, "I haven't bothered anybody. Neither have my friends. I don't know what they're talking about. We always talk and sure, sometimes we laugh while we're studying. We've always done that in the daytime in here. Why should it be any different at night? They sound paranoid to me. Nobody's laughing at them." More students echo the same sentiments. Finally one student says, "I don't care if they use this place, but I certainly expect to use it too. I have just as much right to use it as they do. My parents are taxpayers, too!"

The encounter of the two groups described here was taken from a real situation. Resolution of the conflict was reached after a lengthy discussion that followed the procedures given above. The discussion was successfully moderated by the librarian. The method used to reach resolution required that each group stay together until they could reach consensus as to what should be done to insure fair treatment for everyone. The solutions of both groups were compared, and a common solution reached. Once the idea that everyone did indeed have a right to use the library was firmly established, the two groups found that only two rules needed to be accepted. The first required quiet for study and reading with no loud talking or other noise allowed in the Circulation Room during the evening hours. This rule was in contrast to the general daytime climate of the room, which was relatively noisy and busy. In the daytime, students chose the room to work together, do homework, or talk and relax. They had access to the Reference Room across the hall as an alternate choice if they needed absolute silence. In the evening, because of lack of staff to supervise, the Reference Room was open only on request for materials and not available for study. Since day students were not required to be in the library in the evening, but rather came there by choice, they were asked to respect the adults' need for a quiet climate. Anyone talking out loud or deliberately being noisy would be asked to use the library during daytime hours only.

The second rule stated that no abusive gestures or behavior would be tolerated. People who offended others would be asked to leave immediately on the first offense and if, on returning another time, they repeated such behavior they would be asked not to return for the school year.

The establishment of these rules pleased all but a tiny faction within each group; however, everyone agreed to abide by the rules. The rules are still in effect three years later and no further incidents have occurred.

From the tiniest rural library to the largest university or public library system, every library and librarian must be concerned about groups. Whether it is the board of trustees, "Friends of the Library" volunteers, a class of students learning library skills, the local environmental conservation club that meets weekly in the library, the professional library association, or the library staff, groups and groupness are a part of all libraries. Librarians will inevitably be members of one or more groups. In many cases, they will assume leadership roles. They will also be concerned with other groups, such as city government, whose responsibilities or goals regularly affect library programs in some way. Knowledge of group dynamics can help librarians understand the intricacies and vagaries of the behaviors, feelings, attitudes, and values involved. Armed with such understanding, librarians can play a more effective role as members or leaders of groups and can help group members interact with one another more successfully.

An Overview

That much of contemporary life goes on within the changing contextual arrangements of groups is evident. Indeed, the amount of time people spend doing things together in groups is considerable. Most people simultaneously belong to family groups, learning groups, work groups, peer groups, social-recreational groups, and so forth. No wonder, then, that they sometimes find their collective heads spinning as they attempt to make sense out of the ever-changing patterns of membership and the apparently bewildering number of possible configurations of groups. Add to this the fact that the functioning or malfunctioning of groups is increasingly recognized as a major societal problem, and it becomes obvious that groups are a central and complex aspect of today's world. "Neither a coherent view of man nor an advanced social technology is possible without dependable answers to a host of questions concerning the operations of groups, how individuals relate to groups, and how groups relate to larger society" (Cartwright and Zander, 1968, p. 4).

Historically, a great deal of wisdom about the nature of groups, the relations between individuals and groups, and the ways to manage group life can be found in early philosophical writing. European literature from the sixteenth through the nineteenth centuries featured impressive speculations on the nature of man and his place in society. In the twentieth century, group dynamics as a field of study developed into the integrated body of knowledge and procedures in use today.

Group dynamics recognizes that common principles and processes cut across all groups regardless of their characteristics or tasks. Its development in part stemmed from intellectual curiosity, in part, from a desire to improve social conditions and social practices. By the mid-1930s, cultural, economic, social, and intellectual conditions were favorable. The democratic belief that people and society could be improved and the value placed on science, technology, progress, and rational problem solving demanded answers to questions and problems involving groups and their relationships. It is significant, given the belief and the feasibility of the study of social problems so evident in the conditions described above, that the Society for the Psychological Study of Social Issues was established in 1936.

What had happened? Several trends converged in the 1930s. First, social group workers were abundant. They were committed to the notion that groups could be managed so as to bring about changes in individual members. Second, a separate branch of psychiatry following ideas on groups set forth by Freud, Bion, and Moreno was using groups for therapeutic purposes. Third, influenced greatly by Dewey, American education endeavored not only to transmit knowledge, but also to prepare people for life in society. Teachers were interested in instilling skills of leadership, cooperation, responsible membership, and human relations within the context of the classroom group. Fourth, administrators of all types were greatly affected by studies of the social organization of work groups and of the interpersonal relations networks within the work setting.

Equally as important was the maturation of the social sciences. They had progressed from the era of the "group mind" and the "collective unconscious," through the debate over whether groups, institutions, and cultures have a reality apart from the individuals who participate in them or whether individuals alone have a reality and groups represent abstractions from collections of individuals, to the development of empirically based research techniques that opened the way for scientific study. From experiments on individuals and groups, from controlled observation of social interaction, and from sociometric rating procedures, the social sciences moved to the experimental creation of social norms (Sherif, 1936), the study of the social base of attitudes (Newcomb, 1943), the social organization and influence of street corner groups (Whyte, 1943), to the experimental manipulation of group atmosphere (Lewin, Lippitt, and White, 1939; Lippit, 1940). These last two studies represent a major synthesis of the various trends and developments through the 1930s and the beginnings of modern group dynamics.

What, then, is a group? There are a number of available definitions. Homans argued that "a group is defined by the interaction of its members" (1950, p. 84). The sociological concept of a group was represented by Merton as "a number of people who interact with one another in accord with established patterns" (1957, p. 285). Newcomb stated, "the distinctive thing about a group is that it's members share norms about something" (1951, p. 33). Bass defined a group "as a collection of individuals whose existence as a collection is rewarding to the individuals" (1960, p. 39). Gibb (1964) defined a group as a collection of interacting persons with some degree of reciprocal influence over one another. Lewin (1948) stressed the importance of social interaction and other types of interdependence. In line with Lewin, Cartwright and Zander offered the following definition: "[a] group is a collection of individuals who have relations to one another that make them interdependent to some significant degree" (p. 46).

These definitions clearly indicate that a group can be defined in a number of different ways, focusing on a number of different dimensions. For the purposes of this chapter, a group is defined as a collection of interacting individuals who have come together to work on a common task and who, in the process of this work, influence each other in some way.

The basic issues of group dynamics or group processes (this latter term is used interchangeably with the former) are numerous and variable. Depending on where a person might stake his theoretical claim, some issues become more important than others. The authors do not wish to argue for any one model at the expense of any other; thus, they are emphasizing, without a particular theoretical bias, the following issues or dimensions: (1) the informal and formal aspects of group life; (2) the task and socioemotional (i.e., content and process) components; (3) expectations; (4) leadership; (5) attraction; (6) norms; (7) communication; (8) cohesiveness; and (9) the sequences of group development (e.g., linear, helical, and cyclical). Before continuing, the reader is referred to two classic resources in the area: Cartwright and Zander's *Group Dynamics* and Schmuck and Schmuck's *Group Processes in the Classroom* (1975). These will provide more detail on the following material.

1. *Informal and formal aspects of a group:* A constant ebb and flow of pressure and influence occurs between the formal and the informal in any group (Cooley, 1956). Formal aspects refer to the ways in which members work as they carry out the specific goals of the group. Some examples of the formal are roles and role requirements, stated purposes of the group, and desired end products. Informal aspects refer to individually specific ways in which members view and relate to other members as people. Some examples of the informal are affection, friendship patterns, and level of intimacy. The formal and informal reciprocally influence each other. Research (e.g., the Hawthorne studies; Rothlisberger and Dickson, 1939) has pointed out the importance of informal relationships in work groups for productivity and for a number of other dimensions. Clearly then, informal, affective relations among people are inevitable in any group. Failure to take these into consideration may result in unnecessary difficulties at the formal level.

2. *Task and socioemotional components of a group:* All interpersonal situations involve an unavoidable, affective component. Within a group context this plays a vital and powerful role. The tendency is for most groups to concentrate on the task at hand, the content of the group. Yet socioemotional forces are in operation that have little or nothing to do with the task. These affective processes impact the ways in which members can and do work on any task. For example, harsh and unexplained feelings may develop between a leader and the members. Similarly, problems in communication may occur although the task is clear and the language precise. Bion (1959) referred to these underlying emotional patterns as basic assumptions. His notion held that in every group two groups are actually present, the task group and the basic assumption group. Whereas the task is overt, the basic assumptions are covert. The basic assumptions constitute a group's *hidden agenda*. This

agenda forces the group to behave as if a certain assumption is basic to its maintenance, growth, and survival. Bion offered three types of basic assumptions. First, dependency—in which a group seeks support from a person or a thing that members see as stronger and more powerful than themselves. Second, fight-flight—in which survival is contingent upon fighting the task or fleeing from it. Both fight and flight occur as concomitants of the work of the group. Third, pairing—in which members join one another in ever-changing patterns of twos in order to cope with problems or to increase personal satisfaction.

These underlying socioemotional forces or basic assumptions are oriented inward, not outward toward the task. The work group requires concentration, skill, organization of its resources, and cooperation from its members. The basic assumption group, since it is necessary for survival, exists without effort.

3. *Interpersonal expectations:* An interpersonal expectation is a prediction of how another person will behave. It is commonly accepted that people develop expectations for themselves and for others with whom they interact over a period of time. What is becoming more and more understood and accepted is that such expectations can not only influence what they see in others, but also cause certain things or events to happen. These interpersonal expectations (also known as the Pygmalion effect or the self-fulfilling prophecy) result from a number of different factors. These include sex, age, clothing style, race, family backgrounds, history, cumulative records, data, and so forth. They are important in that they influence group processes and expectations of group productivity.

4. *Leadership:* The search for the special personality characteristics of a leader has failed to yield any convincing results. Leadership seems to be a situational variable. Within this context several factors have been identified. These include the ability to sense or to be aware of what is going on in oneself as well as in others, the skill and competence to make a contribution to the task of the group and to the emotional processes of the group and the nature of the task itself. Essentially, leadership is a set of behaviors that helps the group move toward its objectives. In a pioneer study on leadership, Lewin, Lippitt, and White found that (*a*) *autocratic* and *laissez-faire* groups were not as original in their work as *democratic* groups; nor was *autocracy* more efficient than *democracy;* (*b*) more dependence and less individuality was noted in the *autocratic* groups; (*c*) more friendliness and group-mindedness resulted under *democratic* leaders; and (*d*) under *autocratic* leaders, more overt and covert hostility and aggression occurred. In line with these results, qualities in followers may indeed influence their choice

of leadership. More specifically, more authoritarian people might well demand strong direction by a single person, while more egalitarian people are apt to want and to value leaders who are responsive to the feelings of individuals. Tannenbaum (1968) found that satisfaction of followers is related to their perception of the degree to which they can influence decision making, as well as to the kind of influence their leader has over them. Thus leadership is clearly a complex variable, more complex than had been assumed in the past.

5. *Attraction:* People need closeness with other people and they need people with whom they feel secure and comfortable. Without affiliation, feelings of loneliness, worthlessness, and anxiety may arise to prevent maximum use of any person's potential. That the small group plays a role in terms of development of attraction and good feelings, and that good feelings and attraction play a role in the development of the group, point to the reciprocal nature of group processes and attraction.

6. *Norms:* Norms are shared expectations or attitudes about what appropriate procedures and behaviors are. They are strong stabilizers of behavior. They are vital for group development and group functioning, and are oftentimes crucial maintainers of group behavior and direction. Norms are strong stabilizers because group members monitor each other's behaviors on the basis of identified and accepted norms. A group norm arises out of two forces: (*a*) forces within the individual to reduce conflict felt when personal actions are different from those held by others; and (*b*) forces induced by others who wish to influence the person's behavior. An understanding of norms is crucial for an understanding of mainstream behavior and deviant behavior.

7. *Communication:* Both verbal and nonverbal communication are the vehicles by which group processes occur. Within the context of a group, communication occurs through information sharing, problem solving, norming, decision making, and conflict resolution. Indeed all of these processes are subprocesses of communication. Different communication patterns and procedures are available in all groups. The particular pattern or procedure selected is in part dependent on the nature of the group's task and its membership's expectations and values.

8. *Cohesiveness:* Group cohesiveness refers to the degree to which the members of the group desire to remain in the group. It results from two sets of forces acting on members: (*a*) those arising from the attractiveness of the group; and (*b*) those arising from the attractiveness of other groups. Cohesiveness is a highly researched aspect of group dynamics. Many studies have been undertaken to ascertain the conditions that bring about various levels of cohesiveness. Others have investigated the effects of different levels of cohesiveness on the group,

on its members, and on the group's performance. Even though it is widely researched, it remains somewhat of an enigma because of its circularity.

9. *Developmental models of groups:* All human groups are changing. Having lives of their own, the primary characteristic of groups is movement. Different models of group development exist. For the purposes of this chapter the linear model, which regards change as a progressive, straight line function over a time, is the best simple model for use in the library. In a group-development theory, content, process, and structure are closely interrelated. *Content* is what is being said and is determined by the group's task. *Process* refers to how a group behaves and functions. *Structure* includes the leader's attitude and theory, the group's objectives, norms, contracts, and ground rules. To a lesser extent it also refers to the environment.

Education and Group Dynamics

It is hoped that librarians will view themselves as educators/facilitators while reading this material and that they will consider the material that follows useful to any person working in a "helping" profession. For those who teach, in the formal sense of that word, much of what is included here may already be familiar, but viewed in the context of this book it may take on wider implications.

The most important book the authors have found about education and group dynamics is *Group Processes in the Classroom* by Richard and Patricia Schmuck (1975). It offers a summary of the basic dynamics that affect learning and working together successfully, as well as some specific interpretations (that relate to the general theory) of research done on classes as groups. While there are obvious differences between and among schools and libraries and between and among teachers and librarians, the information concerning group dynamics, some of which Schmuck and Schmuck have extrapolated from general research and applied to classrooms, is equally applicable and pertinent not only to class groups but also to task forces, planning committees, staff meetings, in-service sessions, and literary/media discussion groups. The more specific studies done by Schmuck and Schmuck on classroom dynamics are legitimate subjects for study by librarians.

Lest they be accused of oversimplification, the authors urge the reader to study carefully the entire work of Schmuck and Schmuck. Only those highlights that relate to the other subjects discussed in this book and that share a common philosophy with some of the other communication models are introduced here.

Schmuck and Schmuck emphasized *process*, the factors that influence not only the stated goals of the group and the ways in which the group goes about reaching such goals, but also the hidden world of emotional life that is part of every individual and every group. The processes involve: (1) individual members' expectations of themselves and of others; (2) leadership and the uses and abuses of power; (3) members' needs for inclusion and feelings of affiliation—their attraction for one another; (4) the norms and group attitudes and how the range of norms affect the goals of the group; (5) affective and cognitive communication skills; (6) the cohesiveness of the group; (7) the sequential tasks of development of the group as they work together; and (8) the influence of the total governing organization (university, school, hospital, city government, etc.) on the group as it progresses in its work together with the organization. Each of these components will be examined more closely, particularly those that have not been previously discussed.

Individual Expectations

According to Schmuck and Schmuck, members of a group should know that expectations influence the participants' success or lack of success on a task, their sense of self-esteem, as well as their social status or position within the group. Each member should be aware of the expectations she holds for each individual in a group, as well as for the group as a whole. A member should also understand that her own expectations will influence the ways in which she behaves toward the individuals in the group. She should seek ways to check on her own behavior toward others, and should seek out information to better understand each member in the group. She should be receptive to correcting and tailoring her own expectations and behavior as a result of learning more about individuals in the group.

Leadership

Schmuck and Schmuck maintain that a leader should be aware that all people participating in a group need to feel that they have some impact, some influence in dealing with the significant people in their lives. They need to feel competent (White, 1959). For that reason the more diffused the leadership is—the more people actually involved and successful in sharing and carrying out leadership tasks—the more successful the group is likely to be.

Leadership studies have shown that expert and referent power are two of the most successful ways to influence and guide people within a group. Expert power comes with knowledge and expertise in a given area. Referent power carries with it the ability to stimulate others, to feel close to or identify with the leader. Although not always acknowledged, the least effective power is that which uses coercion, punishment, or even rewards! Goal-directed influence, that which stimulates participants in a group to develop autonomous self-initiated work, facilitates learning. This is more likely to be realized when leadership is dispersed or shared in the group, rather than held by one person.

Attraction

As stated above, all group participants need to be attractive to someone else within the group. Friendship and acceptance by peers enables a learner to perform better intellectually. In fact the social behavior within the group, interestingly enough, has the most influence on how attractive an individual may be even in a learning group. Although intelligence, as well as physical attributes and mental health, may also be factors, they too are influenced by the social behavior of the individual. For example, being very bright may be considered offensive if it manifests itself through supercilious, antisocial, or bizarre behavior that makes others feel uncomfortable. Some of the simplest facts (and perhaps most readily accepted as true) need repeating here. People are attracted to those who respect and like them and who give them a sense of well being. They tend to avoid people who make them feel unimportant and defensive. People tend to return favorable comments and behavior with similar complimentary responses, and negative comments and behavior with unfavorable, uncomplimentary responses. The relationships of individuals within a group are an integral part of what happens in terms of tasks and goals. Perhaps not quite so well known but equally important is the fact that a group that has dispersed friendships, where everyone has at least one or more friends and there are few animosities, has a greater opportunity for success than a group where a few people are highly popular and a number of people are without friends.

Norms

Viewed from the point of view of the learning group, Schmuck and Schmuck emphasized that if peer group norms differ from the norms and goals of the professional organization (school, library, etc.), individuals within the group may challenge the professional norms and goals and the end result may be lack of success in learning or benefiting from association with the group.

Behavioral norms might be only superficially adopted in some cases—not truly accepted, but used instead as a sort of protective coloration against rejection. Fear of rejection, if such norms are violated, may be so intense (particularly for adolescents) that "pluralistic ignorance" (Schmuck and Schmuck, p. 19) comes into play. This is the phenomenon that occurs when an individual develops fallacious reasoning, poor judgment, and incorrect perceptions of the way things really are. "I can't study in the Reference Room because my friends will think I'm an intellectual snob or a 'brown nose!' "

Communication

Since elsewhere in this book various problems in communication have been addressed, it should be sufficient to state here that Schmuck and Schmuck emphasize the importance of developing openness, skills in listening, disclosure, and confrontation as well as concern for others, for maximum success in the learning group.

Cohesiveness

Cohesiveness is the state of togetherness that results from members of the group feeling that they are included, needed, and involved. Cohesiveness may be recognized by the verbalizations and the actions of a group. Use of the word "we" in reference to a group is significant. Statements of a sense of well-being resulting from group activities show that a group has cohesiveness. In some cases, social patterns that carry over after group meetings also indicate cohesiveness. For the learning group to be attractive, members must find that they can derive a sense of achievement, a sense of power, and a sense of belonging by being part of the group. Learning is most likely to occur in groups that are highly cohesive, if the norms of the group support academic involvement and achievement. The success of a cohesive learning group also depends on interpersonal expectations, leadership patterns, attractiveness of members to each other, and communication skills. In a sense, all of the above ingredients of groupness are interdependent upon each other and cannot really be separated from each other.

Sequential Stages of Development of a Group

Human groups are changing all the time. One important theory that describes the evolution of group behavior was developed by Schutz (1958, 1966). His theory was based on the notion that three emotional needs of group members (i.e., Inclusion, Control, and Affection) play an important and sequential role in the group's life. In the first stage of a group's life, members will concentrate on finding a place for themselves. What part will each person play? Who will recognize that person and accept her as a part of the group? Once accepted, a person will then test her influence on and control of decisions made by the group and will test the degree of her individual responsibility to the group. This is a period that involves power struggles that continue until some kind of comfortable balance is achieved, with each member knowing where she fits in the scheme of things. Finally the members of the group turn to the emotional issue of affection, with each person seeking a level of intimacy necessary for real comfort within the group. If members can fulfill each other's affection needs, they are more likely to operate successfully and cooperatively in accomplishment of tasks.

Governing Organization

The influence of the governing organization on any group, whether a university, a public school, a hospital, or a city government, is highly complex. Such influence develops from the formal and informal relations among staff and other persons who are connected with or use the services of the organization, and also from the facilities, program, philosophy, goals, work schedules, budget, etc., of the organization. If the parent organization's impact upon the group is important, the anthropological view—that is, a way of viewing the group as part of an entire culture—is thus significant, particularly when a group is seeking to change itself in relationship to the governing organization. A detailed discussion of the anthropological view is beyond the scope of this book. To explore further ways in which this culture influences organizations and some of the problems encountered when organizations attempt change within established cultural patterns, the authors recommend the work of Sarason (1971, 1972).

The following case studies are offered as a means for the reader to investigate more about groups and how they relate to library service. They may assist the reader in analyzing the components of group life and group behavior.

Case Study No. 1

Our curriculum has prepared us in our subject expertise so we know the materials. Important also is an ability to perform with young adults in *loco amici*, sometimes even *amicus curiae*, if no longer in *loco parentis*. [Lillian L. Shapiro in *Serving Youth; Communication and Commitment in the High School Library* (New York: R. R. Bowker, 1975), p. 6.]

One of the most challenging experiences in teaching within the library is helping a class of outwardly indifferent students find the materials they need for a project. On this particular occasion, a teacher had planned with the librarian to bring a small class of "slow learners" to the media center for a project that had been used successfully with another class the year before. The librarian was forewarned, however, that these particular students were not confident that they could do any of the work suggested in the project. The objectives were for the students to find information on Conrad Richter's *Light in the Forest* (New York: Knopf, 1953), to locate descriptions of various related Indian life styles, to find historical background information on white American settlers of that day, and to find biographical and critical materials on the author. The unit began with a great deal of complaining by the students that this was much too hard and that they could not possibly do all that was asked. Since the assignment was set up in contract style, which allowed a minimum amount of work for a passing grade, the teacher felt sure that most of her students would make an attempt to do some, if not all, of the work.

The teacher and the librarian each began by moving from table to table encouraging everyone to begin. At one of the first tables the librarian found three students sitting glumly immobile. They had no intention of doing any work at all. She sensed that they wanted her to do it for them. Although she felt concerned about their lack of energy, she sat beside them and suggested that they were "shortchanging" themselves and that she knew they could do the work if they wanted to. Since she knew one of the students, she focused some of her attention on him and implied that he could definitely help the others. She called him by name and kidded with him so that the others could see that she had had some contact with him previously. Eventually he responded and made his way, if somewhat reluctantly, to the card catalog. The others eventually followed him.

Some time later when the librarian checked back to see how they were doing she saw that they had located some material, but that they were obviously disappointed in it. One student looked up and said, "There's nothing in this place. This stuff is no good. I'll have to go to the public library to get anything done." The librarian knew that they were confirming their own negative expectations and so she said, "Well look, you've already found something; I'm sure you can find some more. Don't put yourself down, now. You're going to do just fine." The boy responded, "It's too late now anyway. The period is almost over. I'll just have to go to the public library. This place stinks."

Rather than rise to the bait, the librarian simply said, "See you tomorrow," and walked away.

The following day the student returned with a book from the public library. His two friends huddled beside him, each looking as discouraged as they had the day before. The librarian approached immediately, saying, "Good, I see you have found some more material. You were really resourceful. Some kids wouldn't have bothered to go all the way to the public library. I'm sure you can do a good job here, too. I'll be back in a minute with some more materials for you."

Since she knew by now that they had chosen to deal with Indian dwellings, she located a book that had excellent information and particularly good illustrations on that aspect of Indian culture. She brought back the book and carefully pointed out examples suitable for their use. Then she left the table after a few more encouraging words.

For the rest of the week she worked with other students in the class using much the same approach—always consciously up-beat in manner, particularly when students put themselves down. The teacher, who had been somewhat skeptical about most of the students, had deliberately offered extra incentive. She too continued to offer positive feedback whenever and wherever she could.

At the end of the week, when the project was nearly completed, the student who had complained about the library swaggered up to the circulation desk and announced to the librarian, "This place is OK. Just like you said, I found plenty of stuff. So did the others in my group." The project, which had seemed doomed to failure, ended with everyone having done something and with most feeling like they had done their fair share of work. Both the teacher and librarian were satisfied with the students' participation. And the quality of the work done was better than they had hoped for.

Case Study No. 2

At last, everybody had arrived. The committee had been waiting not quite patiently for over an hour. Nick Jones, the chairman of the design committee, had wondered silently if the delay was a portent of things to come. He had not really wanted to chair the committee. But Adrianne Booth, the head librarian, had been very persuasive. She had indicated that the committee, which was to draw up the final plans for the new and long-awaited public library, needed a young, aggressive, and innovative librarian as its head. Ferde Boaz, an architect with a number of public buildings to his credit, had been delayed because of another project. That in itself would not have been so bad, but he had canceled out three times before due to his other commitments. This one-day session was originally scheduled for six weeks ago, and they had a nine-month deadline staring them in the face. Nick called the meeting to order. At least now they could begin.

The members of the committee, in addition to Nick and the architect, were representatives of the various library departments—thirteen in all, many of whom did not see eye-to-eye on any issue; two members of the board of trustees; several people from the community; a member of the city council; and Adrianne Booth. Nick viewed his task as difficult, given this mixture, an interesting one to say the least; but the presence of Adrianne, known for her quiet and controlling leadership style, troubled him even more. Why was she on the committee, but not the chairwoman? As the meeting began, Nick swept aside his concern. He had no time to indulge in such "paranoia."

Three reports were scheduled. The first, a site analysis, went fairly well but a bit slowly. Most questions were informational in nature and brief; the answers were to the point and brief also. One hour into the meeting, Nick felt pleased. He had kept the reporter moving and the members on the topic. Maybe this was not going to be so bad, after all.

The second report, a needs survey, began quietly and innocently enough. It presented the thoughts, opinions, and advice of many people representing diverse outlooks and different organizations: librarians, library experts, administrators, the local businessmen's association, private individuals—both those who used the library and those who did not, the local women's club, school officials, university faculty members, politicians, community planners, media manufacturers, publishers, clearing-house representatives, construction specialists, and others. All had different needs.

As the presentation ambled on, the committee members sat quietly; some looked involved, others bored, and still others upset. The data were certainly impressive, but contradictory. After a short but uncomfortable silence, Nick asked if there were any questions or comments. Adrianne Booth commented on the contradictions. Others were quick to follow her lead. Some expressed concern; others excitement. Still others, perceiving themselves as guardians and protectors of materials, expressed cynicism. And still others, hanging on to the past and attempting to preserve an age-old image of the library, expressed strong caution.

Nick attempted to summarize the needs in terms of openness versus security, accessibility versus protection, personal interests versus group interests, public interest versus librarians' interest, efficiency versus involvement, quality of service versus quantity of service. His summary was greeted with an anxious silence. Several committee members looked furtively at Adrianne. But she sat quietly with Sphinx-like reserve. Nick groped for something, anything to say or to do. He was painfully aware of the mounting tension and frustration. He asked if any others cared to organize the needs in a way different from his. No one stepped forward. The half-hearted discussion that ensued wandered aimlessly, at times focusing on the contradictions and at other times ever so briefly touching on the members' feelings. The morning session limped to a close.

Over half the members were late for the start of the afternoon session. The discussion continued unfocused. Moreover, a number of subgroups began to form and carry on their own tangential discussions. Nick's attempts to bring together the various discussions were only partially and temporarily successful. Adrianne was of little or no help. As the afternoon wore on, people became more and more on edge. Tempers began to flare for some, while others withdrew.

Finally someone rose to announce that what was happening was getting the committee nowhere. Another person added that she hoped the meetings were not going to be so disorganized during the remaining months. If it were to be so, she opined that the community would never see the new library. And another person demanded that Nick take charge and lay down some ground rules. Adrianne suggested that the committee adopt a modified parliamentary procedure. A number of people agreed. Some, however, objected to it on the grounds that it would limit, if not stifle, creative ideas and discussion. Eventually the suggestion was brought to a vote. It passed by an overwhelming margin. At last, Nick thought, some work will get done. He was soon to find out that he was wrong.

Several members bowed out of the evening session because of other pressing commitments. Ferde Boaz gave his report, one of the three mentioned above. His eloquent presentation on the principles of architectural design and on the relationship of design to libraries fell on ears somewhat deafened by the day-long confusion and disorder. He left immediately after finishing, promising to attend future meetings when it was possible to do so. Thus, the first planning day drew to a close with the data still replete with contradictions, with the issues still unclarified, with little or no progress made toward a tentative, let alone a final, design, and with frustration evident both toward other members and toward the planning process.

The committee was scheduled to meet biweekly. It did so. The meetings continued in a parliamentary format, but with minimal movement toward the goal. The first overt indication of the extent of its difficulties was the resignation of several members. The second overt sign of trouble was Nick's resignation as chairman. He told the committee that he felt out of his element as a leader since he had no training and very few skills in this area. He also admitted feeling that he had alienated several members with his indecisiveness and his inability to take charge. Adrianne stepped in as chairwoman. She met with a bit more success, but only a bit more.

Over nine months the committee experienced a 52 percent turnover rate. Although Adrianne managed to continue as chairwoman, she did so with much frustration and with a noticeable loss of prestige. Ferde Boaz attended the meetings when he could. He always brought with him a set of tentative designs based in part on what he heard at or was told about previous meetings. These were typically greeted with a combination of admiration, astonishment, and reservation.

At the "eleventh hour" a final design was accepted by the committee. Adrianne presented it to the board of trustees. After several delays and modifications, it was approved. When the library is completed, it will stand as a monument more to the committee's persistence than to its success or creativity.

AN EXERCISE

Observing Group Process

Three observation guides have been provided to highlight group dynamics and hone skills in observing group process. The reader is asked to do two things with them. First, use the guides to review the opening scene of this chapter and the two case studies. Second, use them to map out interactions in the next small group in which you participate (e.g., staff meeting, planning group, ad hoc committee, etc.).

Observation Guide No. 1

TASK FUNCTIONS

Who does these tasks? Are some left undone? Others done too often? Too little? How does each of these tasks affect group success or failure? What might you do about it?

1. Initiating—proposing tasks or goals; defining a group problem; suggesting a procedure; suggesting other ideas for consideration.
2. Information or opinion seeking—requesting facts on problems; seeking relevant information; asking for suggestions or ideas.
3. Information or opinion giving—offering facts; providing relevant information; stating a belief; giving suggestions or ideas.
4. Clarifying or elaborating—interpreting or reflecting ideas or suggestions; clearing up confusion; indicating alternatives and issues; giving examples.

5. Summarizing—putting related ideas together; restating suggestions.
6. Consensus testing—sending up "trial balloons" to see if the group is nearing a conclusion; checking to see how much agreement has been reached.

MAINTENANCE/PROCESS FUNCTIONS

1. Encouraging—being friendly, warm, and responsive to others; accepting others and their contributions; listening.
2. Expressing group feelings—sensing feeling, mood, and relationships; exploring these; sharing personal feelings with the group.
3. Harmonizing—attempting to reconcile disagreements; reducing tension; getting people to explore their differences.
4. Compromising—offering to compromise position, ideas, or status; admitting error(s); disciplining self to help maintain the group.
5. Gate-keeping—seeing that others have a chance to speak; keeping the discussion a group discussion rather than a one, two, or three-way conversation.
6. Setting standards—expressing criteria that will help the group to achieve; applying these in evaluating group function and production.

Listed in figure 6 are the task and maintenance functions performed by various group members. Consider each category, then check the appropriate columns.

Task	*Self*	*Others*	*Leader*
Initiating			
Seeking information or opinion			
Giving information or opinion			
Clarifying or elaborating			
Summarizing			
Consensus testing			

Maintenance/Process

Encouraging			
Expressing group feelings			
Harmonizing			
Compromising			
Gate-keeping			
Setting Standards			

Figure 6.   Task and Maintenance Functions for Group Interaction

Observation Guide No. 2

There are forces or basic assumptions active in all groups that disturb work. These represent a kind of emotional underworld, an undercurrent in the stream of group life. These underlying emotional issues produce a variety of behaviors that interfere with or are destructive to effective group functioning. They cannot be ignored or wished away. They must be recognized and commented on. As the group develops, conditions must be created that permit these issues to be resolved and channeled in the direction of group effort.

THE ISSUES
1. Identity—Who am I in this group? Where do I fit in? What kind of behavior is acceptable here?
2. Goals and needs—What do I want from the group? Can the group goals be made consistent with my goals? What have I to offer to the group?
3. Power, control, and influence—Who will control what I do? How much power and influence do I have?
4. Intimacy—How close will we get to each other? How personal? How can we achieve a greater level of trust?

BEHAVIORS PRODUCED IN RESPONSE TO THESE ISSUES
1. Dependency-counterdependency—leaning on or resisting anyone in the group who represents authority, especially the leader.
2. Withdrawing—trying to remove the sources of uncomfortable feelings by leaving the group, physically and/or psychologically.
3. Fighting and controlling—asserting personal dominance, attempting to get own way regardless of others.
4. Pairing up—seeking out one or two supporters and forming an emotional subgroup for protection and for support.

Listed in figure 7 are the interfering behaviors. Consider each, then check the appropriate columns.

	Self	*Others*
Dependency-counterdependency		
Withdrawing		
Fighting and controlling		
Pairing up		

Figure 7. Interfering Behaviors That Affect Group Interaction

Observation Guide No. 3

Questions for the observer or guest at a group meeting:

1. How did you find out about the group? Are there special requirements for a member?
2. What are the group's stated goals?
3. Is the group's emphasis on cognitive or affective needs?
4. What are the basic assumptions of the group?
5. What are the group's activities? Are either questionable behavior or abusive language a part of the group's activities? Are these encouraged by the leaders? If so, can these be justified by the goals and basic assumptions of the group?
6. Is there a hidden agenda for the group?
7. What are the credentials of those leading or responsible for the meetings of the group? Academic? Work experience? Apprenticeship served with whom? Affiliation with organizations?
8. How does the leader view change?
9. Are there group norms for behavior to which all of the members must conform? Are there exceptions? If one wishes to withdraw or to pass on a particular activity or session, may one do so without embarrassment? Are members free to leave at any time they wish?
10. Is there undue or overwhelming pressure to join the group?
11. Where does the power lie within the group? What kinds of power are used? How does this affect the autonomy and sense of responsibility of individual members? Is there a "guru" type of leader?
12. Does the group have a method of evaluating itself? In terms of process? In terms of task?
13. Does the group have a special or exclusive vocabulary? If so, is that a limiting factor in accomplishing the goals of the group?
14. Is money needed for participation in sessions or for membership? Is this a reasonable sum relative to one's budget and to the time and expertise involved? How is the money used? If there is a fee is it stated openly at the beginning? Is there a budget plan available (i.e., an ability-to-pay scale?)
15. Is secretiveness or confidentiality built into the format? The procedures? The content of the meetings? If so, is it justifiable?

Questions for the individual member:

1. What are your personal/professional goals in joining the group? Do these goals conflict with the goals of the group? Is the group helping you to meet your goals?

2. Do you have sufficient control over your own feelings and behavior when in the group?
3. Do you feel you can maintain your integrity in the face of the group's demands for a certain set of responses?
4. Are the skills, knowledge, or support you derive from the group transferable to the real world?
5. What are the patterns of friendship or support in the group? Do you feel comfortably included?
6. Are members open and honest with one another?
7. Is the group fragmented or united? If fragmented, do you know why?
8. Is there another group in which you might better meet your personal, professional goals?

Those readers interested in group leadership skills may wish to refer to: (1) Leland P. Bradford's *Making Meetings Work* (1976); (2) Michael Doyle and David Straus's *How to Make Meetings Work* (1976); and (3) Norman R. F. Maier's *Problem-Solving Discussions and Conferences: Leadership Methods and Skills* (1963).

References

Bass, Bernard M. *Leadership, psychology, and organizational behavior.* New York: Harper, 1960.

Bion, Wilfred R. *Experiences in groups.* New York: Basic Books, 1959.

Bradford, Leland P. *Making meetings work.* La Jolla, Calif.: University Associates, 1976.

Cartwright, Dorwin, and Zander, Alvin. *Group dynamics: Research and theory.* New York: Harper & Row, 1968.

Cooley, Charles H. *Human nature and the social order.* New York: Free Press, 1956.

Doyle, Michael, and Straus, David. *How to make meetings work.* New York: Wyden, 1976.

Gibb, Jack. Climate for trust formation. In J. Gibb and K. Benne (eds.), *T-group theory and laboratory method.* New York: John Wiley, 1964, 279–309.

Homans, George C. *The human group.* New York: Harcourt, Brace, 1950.

Lewin, Kurt. Resolving social conflicts. New York: Harper, 1948.

———, Lippitt, Ronald, and White, R. Patterns of aggressive behavior in experimentally created "social climates." *Journal of Social Psychology,* 1939, *10,* 271–99.

Lippitt, Ronald. An experimental study of authoritarian and democratic group atmospheres. *University of Iowa Studies in Child Welfare,* 1940, *16,* 43–195.

Maier, Norman R. F. *Problem-solving discussions and conferences: Leadership methods and skills.* New York: McGraw-Hill, 1963.

Merton, Robert K. *Social theory and social structure.* Rev. ed. Glencoe, Ill.: Free Press, 1957.

Newcomb, Theodore. *Personality and social change.* New York: Dryden, 1943.

————. Social psychological theory. In J. H. Rohrer and M. Sherif (eds.), *Social psychology at the crossroads,* pp. 31–49. New York: Harper, 1951.

Roethlisberger, F. J., and Dickson, W. J. *Management and the worker.* Cambridge, Mass.: Harvard University Press, 1939.

Sarason, Seymour B. *The creation of settings and the future societies.* San Francisco, Calif.: Jossey-Bass, 1972.

————. *The culture of the school and the problem of change.* Boston: Allyn & Bacon, 1971.

Schmuck, Richard, and Schmuck, Patricia. *Group processes in the classroom.* Dubuque, Iowa: Wm. C. Brown, 1975.

Schutz, Will. *FIRO: A three dimensional theory of interpersonal behavior.* New York: Holt, Rinehart, & Winston, 1958.

————. *The interpersonal underworld.* Palo Alto, Calif.: Science & Behavior Books, 1966.

Sherif, Muzafer. *The psychology of social norms.* New York: Harper, 1936.

Tannenbaum, A. S. *Control in organizations.* New York: McGraw-Hill, 1968.

White, Robert W. Motivation reconsidered: The concept of competence. *Psychological Review,* 1959, *66,* 297–333.

Whyte, William F. *Street corner society.* Chicago: University of Chicago Press, 1943.

The Humanistic Librarian

Toward Confluent Library
Service

The Scene: A small conference room in a high school media center. The
school librarian and the consulting psychologist are discussing the
first session of a six-session in-service program that they have just conducted. Both are aware that something is not quite the way they want it
to be. Each sees the problem from a different vantage point. Both
understand, however, that the process, or the technique of presentation,
affected and will affect the outcome of their efforts.

The in-service program has been designed for a group of seven people
who work in different capacities in a school media center. Some are
professional librarians or media specialists, others are paraprofessionals
or technicians. All have agreed, if somewhat hesitantly, to be a part of
this project to improve staff communication skills. The idea for in-
service comes from the head librarian's master's program in humanistic
psychology. She believes that if she is to embark on a program of self-
improvement and increased awareness of the psychological implications of her work with people, the staff has a right to know about what
she is learning and a right to keep pace with her—if they wish to do so.
Whether they want to or not, they will inevitably be affected by the
changes in her behavior, her attitudes, and her values as she becomes
more knowledgeable and more skilled in this area. She hopes that they
will see the importance of improving their own communication skills
and their own awareness of the affective needs of the students and the

teachers with whom they work. She also realizes they may view her asking them to take part in a project of self-improvement as a criticism of their present performance, as a threatening or evaluative action, even though she has in the past and continues at present to assure people that this is not so.

She is right. Talking over the process and results of the first session, the psychologist and the librarian agree that some people are distinctly uncomfortable with sharing information about themselves and their co-workers. Some feel it is unnecessary, saying they already know all there is to know about each other. One worker, when asked to evaluate the first exercises, replied, "I wouldn't know—I'm not a psychiatrist!" Most are not quite as obvious in their discomfort, but one other participant states that she would not reveal any information given to her in confidence. The implication of this remark is that she somehow feels that she would at some time be asked to do so, a misunderstanding of the real situation. The librarian and the psychologist have never worked together before in quite this way. They both have been involved in group work where participants attended because of their own desire for self-improvement, rather than at the request of their supervisor. In those situations people are already aware of a need to change their behavior and are taking first steps to do something for themselves. In this situation, however, some of the staff seem to feel that they do not need to change. Also they appear not to be aware of their possible complacency or of the need for growth. Perhaps they simply do not care to become involved in enlarging their responsibilities to the people with whom they work or in changing the affective dimensions of their interactions with people. It has been difficult for them to reveal their true feelings not only because they feel threatened to some degree, but also because they have had no training in affective communication. Skillful confrontation and self-disclosure are behaviors with which they have had little practice.

Discussing the problem further, the psychologist advises the librarian to share her perceptions of what is happening as openly as possible and to allow each person the freedom to bow out gracefully if he or she wishes to do so.

Helping people to deal with change is one of the most difficult tasks that people confront throughout their lives. The administrator or director of a library may wish to see staff members engage in workshops or in-service programs and may find that it is difficult to involve them. The approach used to introduce the idea of self-improvement programs may make or break the success of such a proposal. In other words the process, the techniques of information sharing, discussion, and decision making used with the staff are all-important. The librarian in the open-ing scene might have fared better, for instance, if she had begun by openly sharing her concerns about creating a defensive climate and by providing positive feedback on all staff members' performance. The psychologist, whose understanding of people's reactions to potentially threatening situations was based on wider experience than the librari-an's, might have forewarned her of the need for early disclosure of her own fears.

It is appropriate here, toward the end of the book, that possible feelings of threat be discussed. The authors realize that if they ask readers to change, to do something about the way they deal with them-selves and with others, they may create a defensive climate. The readers are, therefore, referred back to chapter 6 and asked to think carefully about the difference between a supportive and a defensive climate, as described by Jack Gibb. What has been stated here may be interpreted as a kind of evaluation, rather than simply a description, of librarian behavior. The authors may also be perceived as strategizing to change such behavior. Both of these observations are to some extent true; conse-quently they understand that some readers may choose to feel de-fensive.

On the other hand, the authors wish to stress that they care deeply about the readers' feelings and do empathize with librarians, recogniz-ing that their needs are varied and complex (as are all human beings). They do not feel superior or neutral concerning librarians and their relationship to the subject of affective communication; they would never have written this kind of book had that been true. They are taking a risk in sharing what they have learned as they worked together. They ask in turn that the reader also risk carefully considering why such defensive feelings may arise, especially those that may be masked as evaluative criteria for judging this book. There may be a message behind the evaluation that is not understood by the evaluator, one that may have something to do with personal feelings of threat.

The reader may now want to consider taking the following steps to help deal with any feelings of threat that may be subtly lurking, perhaps accompanied by defensive reactions that are not so subtle.

1. Listen to yourself. How do your words connect to your feelings? Are you speaking to relieve or to hide your feelings? Can you describe to yourself how you feel and what you say when you are feeling threatened? Remember you have a choice in saying what you say and also in feeling what you feel. You need not threaten yourself or feel threatened by others. This is a skill, and to be

successful at it you must first learn to recognize when you are feeling threatened. This takes practice as well as honesty.

2. Listen to others empathically. How do their words connect with their feelings? Are they speaking to relieve or to hide their feelings? Could you ask them to describe how they feel or if they are feeling threatened (by you)? How do others respond to what you say? Can you discern when they are feeling threatened by you? Is there more than one response they might make to you? What would those responses be? Would they feel safe saying those things to you? If not, why not?

3. Learn to respond supportively, in nonthreatening ways. (Review Gibb's supportive climates in chapter 6 if necessary.)

4. Incorporate the relatively simple techniques about timing and place that are concerned with disclosure and confrontation. It does matter what you say and how you say it much more, for instance, than simply "getting it off your chest." There is so much more to it than simply saying what "has to be said" whether the other person can take it or not. Choice of words, expression of the voice, positive as well as negative feedback affect the outcome of both disclosure and confrontation, but people are likely to forget such things when they are feeling threatened themselves.

The paradox of communication is that people often erect barriers against openness with each other by use of a particular communication style and then wonder why communication is not effective. The barriers that librarians can erect against open communication are sometimes neatly incorporated into their work. A few of these barriers will be discussed here.

In the Name of Service

In the name of service to people, people themselves are often forgotten. An example of this can be seen in some of the snags that occur in an attempt to share services. Interlibrary loan, for instance, can be and is an unpleasant experience in some systems because the people charged with the responsibility of carrying it out cannot (or will not) tolerate deviation from the norm. Unusual or exceptional requests that do not follow the designated territorial pattern are considered annoying, counterproductive, if not actually inconsiderate. People carrying out requests are not taught to consider the fact that considerable ill-will, frustration, and negative feelings about libraries are generated when interlibrary loan policies are either inflexible or irrational. Instead of viewing each request as unique, considering the personal needs of the individual as well as the needs of the librarian transmitting the request, an unusual demand may be greeted with a lecture on wasted time, or on abuse of the system, and sometimes be accompanied by an outright refusal of help. Unrecognized or ignored is the fact that a verbal dressing down or a cold refusal comes across to another person as a put down, a controlling nonempathic kind of communication. Such behavior provokes defensive reactions on the other's part. Doubtless the librarian in charge of interlibrary loan service does not really intend to trigger that kind of response, but well-intentioned librarians have been known to mar good working relations with other library personnel and the public in just this way. If, in fact, someone consistently abuses a smoothly operating loan system, it might be helpful for staff to inquire with genuine concern as to why the individual persists in a particular approach. Could it possibly be that the system is really not efficient? Might it be improved by the addition of some specific procedural exceptions? Would the resulting good-will be worth the extra detail or work involved?

Interlibrary loan may not, of course, be a problem in many library systems. It has been used here only as an example to point out that cooperative services sometimes go awry because of personal inflexibility or because of a lack of awareness of the importance of the people behind requests for service.

In the Name of Professionalism

Other communication problems can arise as a result of overemphasis on professionalism. Some professionals establish their positions in libraries at the expense of the self-esteem of both individual workers and team cohesiveness and cooperation. For example, particular tasks may be designated as professional only, even when nonprofessional personnel are perfectly capable of learning the work through apprenticeship or in-service training. The very professionals who promote individualized lifetime learning as a goal for everyone may be the first to deny staff members without sanctioned degrees or credentials an opportunity for advancement through any route except the one by which they themselves became certified. This is sometimes known as maintaining professional standards. (Or perhaps as insuring one's own job!) Even though everyone knows exceptionally fine paraprofessionals who have absorbed all there is to know about general reference or beginning classification and cataloging by working with a professional on the job, it is virtually impossible for many of these people to become "professionals" without going to graduate school. Most of them earn so little at their work that they can hardly afford graduate school; thus, they continue to work as paraprofessionals. (Could that be Catch 023.5?)

Worse than the fact that these people may never have an opportunity to earn a professional degree are the polarity and the divisiveness that can develop between professionals and paraprofessionals. Feelings of self-worth are at stake on both sides. Unfortunately there is an unspoken but tacitly acknowledged communication made in such cases that professional librarians are somehow superior in their contributions and their performances, even in their humanity! By dint of sitting in classrooms and earning graduate credit hours their wisdom becomes the only valid type when policies are being discussed or library programs are being planned. It is possible that there are librarians who hold that this is the correct course and that the reactions of paraprofessionals to being kept "in their place" are unimportant. It is entirely possible, however, that changes can be made that would correct the affective climate in such situations, regardless of the number of credit hours available. Respect for one another, shared skills, and common knowledge could become more important than credentials, elitism, and territory.

Elitism that masquerades as professionalism can also divide groups of librarians from each other. Media specialists may think of themselves as superior to audiovisual librarians or school librarians because they are "total media" people. Academic librarians may see themselves as more scholarly, more intellectual because of their association with higher education and academia (they too may suffer from lack of status, refused faculty standing by professors who are engaged in a similar kind of elitism). Public librarians may see themselves as infinitely more important than other librarians because they offer services to the "real world"—all of the people. Male librarians may see themselves as superior to female librarians, and so on and so forth. Such limited and limiting ego-building generally sets up barriers to cooperative ventures. Competition for clientele, funding, jobs, outright rejection of requests for service to each other's clientele, or discounting of each other's expertise may result in real animosities in a community or region where such elitism prevails.

Excuses may be made about time, money, or methods, all of which mask the real problem: "we" versus "them." This can take the form of a subtle operation, in many cases involving people who genuinely believe that there are good reasons for denying, ignoring, or blocking opportunity for cooperation with other groups of librarians. If asked to examine their own motives, the first group may connect their own feelings or attitudes with seemingly legitimate grievances against a second group's ignorance, ill will, or bad faith. Specific examples are often presented as evidence to justify this position. The fact that such specific evidence exists ought not to be an excuse for doing nothing about improving intergroup relationships. In fact, such evidence is all the more reason to examine the process of intergroup communication. Problems are often viewed in terms of the surface content of the issue, becoming a matter of who wins, who loses, and polarity rather than productivity.

In the Name of Communication

"Communication" is generally acknowledged to be a part of all people's work. The word, however, can also convey different connotations than the one used throughout this book. It can become a catchall word, a neat cop-out that explains someone else's failure to share information. "They don't (rather than won't) communicate well" or, "It's a communication problem—not much we can do about it." Examples abound in this area. One that comes to mind was shared with the authors by a woman who works at the circulation desk in a small college library. One day when she answered the phone, she received a request for the starting time for a certain class scheduled in the library that night. She referred to the schedule and responded that there was no class scheduled for that night. Although she tried to refer the person to the Continuing Education Division, he persisted until finally she put the call through to the head librarian. He told the caller what he had neglected to tell his staff: there was, in fact, a class scheduled for the library that night.

In one library alone a multitude of relatively minor communication problems, like the one above, can build into a serious problem. Many times this buildup of minor problems can reach crisis proportions before anyone realizes what is happening. Recently several members of a college faculty described to the authors their desperate attempts to improve communication with the director. They reported that library staff meetings are called only when an individual staff member requests one on an emergency basis. The library director is seldom accessible to the students or to the faculty; he seldom leaves his office and never eats lunch in the faculty dining room. Requests for book orders remain unfilled for months, in some cases for years. Verbal undermining of fellow staff members is common. Peer evaluations are unsigned, severely damaging the confidence of hardworking and respected individuals. Salaries of key workers are below comparable salaries elsewhere on the campus. In short, a critical morale situation exists while the director, like the proverbial ostrich, hides his head, if not in the sand then in the privacy of his secretary-guarded office. People have tried to approach him about all of the above problems. Unfortunately leadership across the board on this campus is sadly lacking. Thus the library director continues to ignore requests for changes and continues to perpetuate a sadly deteriorating situation.

Another example of such communication difficulties occurred recently to one of the authors. In search of information for this book, she visited a number of libraries in the state. In one elementary school library she found only seven or eight children—all of whom had been sent there to be punished. The paraprofessional who was the only person on duty at the time expressed her dismay about having the library used in this way but offered no explanation. The author, feeling that such a practice should not go unchallenged, later phoned the woman in charge of supervising the elementary school libraries of that city. Her concern was greeted with apparent sympathy. It seemed that the author's point of view was shared by the supervisor and that the supervisor was glad to know someone else was concerned. She was duly thanked and told that the matter would be investigated. Several days later the author was informed that the principal of the school was very annoyed with her because she had not spoken directly to him about her concern. He felt he had been ignored in the chain of command. The author had discussed the matter with the person in charge of the library (deliberately beginning at where she believed the chain started), rather than going over the supervisor's head. Now the principal claimed to have been bypassed! In the meantime, the substance of her concern was also being neatly bypassed. The principal was managing to divert attention from the issue by launching a counterattack using the only thing he could find fault with, the author's approach. When the author called the principal to explain why she did what she thought was right, she reiterated her concern about children being forced to go to the library as punishment. She also expressed her concern for his feelings about being bypassed. He simply said that he saw no problem; he felt certain that children had no difficulty in distinguishing between being sent to the library for educational reasons and being sent for punitive ones. It was obvious to her that he was still upset and that he could not discuss the matter objectively. Rather than try to argue with him, she let the whole thing pass as he changed the subject and closed the conversation.

Even when following what one believes to be the courteous or correct procedure, communication problems can be sticky. A problem like the one described may have no simple resolution. Some comfort, however, can be taken in understanding what is really happening and in knowing that one can at least express one's feelings openly. The success of interactions with other professionals depends not only on understanding what is happening, but also on empathizing with the other point of view.

Learning how to deal with one's own feelings, with the feelings of others, and with the communication process is tough enough to warrant serious study. At present, though, the communication process is viewed by some as being too tough to handle, the attitude being if things are left as they are, at least they will not get worse. The authors' point of view, however, is that there is nothing worse in communication than the kinds of miserable towers of Babel presently being constructed. Someone needs to begin to sort it all out. Someone has to be willing to consider piecing together the relevant components of affective communication and semantics so that people can untangle the motives, values conflicts, crossed transactions, games, defensiveness, irresponsibility, processes, unresponsiveness, and unheeding behavior so prevalent today.

The examples provided in this book may seem irrelevant or perhaps too extreme. They may fit one librarian's experience and not another's. Of course there are trouble-free library programs with cooperative, caring personnel in existence everywhere, but everyone needs to evaluate the communication patterns that affect their lives. The defensive person who sees herself beyond the need for such assessment is indeed beyond the help of anyone but herself. Psychology, particularly the humanistic approaches to problem solving and change, may be dismissed as the wrong method, but the authors believe that such dismissals are made out of fear of self-disclosure, fear of failure, and/or fear of the unknown. While such fears are understandable, the authors hope readers will see how self-defeating they can be. The approaches described in this book are offered with understanding of such fears. Everyone is, after all, in the same human lifeboat together and each needs the other. All of the models discussed here have built-in nonthreatening ways of helping people who wish to be helped. Understanding the common threads that are part of all the models will help individuals deal with the complex processes of change.

The shared assumptions underlying the models will provide a foundation for taking the first steps towards changing one's own communicative behavior. The authors caution here, as the separate threads begin to come together and significant points are summarized, that some concepts appear deceptively simple. The reader may have heard them before in some other context; they even may have been labeled simplistic. The authors suggest that it might be helpful to acknowledge that some of the simplist concepts are the most difficult to incorporate in practice. Because the concepts sound familiar does not mean that they have been integrated successfully into the lives of most people. When the authors mentioned in the beginning of the book the need for a fourth basic skill, they were not being facetious. They truly believe that to learn to communicate confluently, considering not only the content of the message but its process, not only the cognitive aspects of the message but the affective implications and impact of the message, is to learn a very difficult but very important and necessary skill. This book was written precisely because they feel so strongly about the importance of communication in everything that people do.

A student of anthropology presently completing his doctoral dissertation at Harvard recently approached one of the authors with a theory he had about change. He stated that he believed the library in a school seemed to be the place where the greatest exchange of all kinds of information took place. The library seemed to him a place where the real changes first occurred in the climate of the school. In disseminating information he was gathering about changing sex roles and career opportunities for young people, he suggested that perhaps the library, with its changing flow of people and information, could be the most effective "change place" in a school and the librarian the most effective "change agent." The authors believe he is right. They also believe that effective change agents exist in public libraries, university libraries, and special libraries. Libraries may be in the forefront of helping to establish new and better communication patterns. For librarians this position is a choice, not something predetermined by fate. It will depend entirely upon the roles librarians themselves choose to take on during the next decade. The authors hope many librarians will decide to use their particular position, their expertise, and their resources to expand their peoplework beyond its present dimensions.

This book may not appear to be interested in asking the reader for intellectual growth, since it is directed primarily at the affective domain. (It is, of course, obvious to the authors that librarians are more than capable of dealing with cognitive matters.) However, the authors would like to stress here that it takes a bit of mind stretching to discover and understand the relationship between the intellect and affect, the left brain and the right brain, and to rethink their connections with one another. It is precisely because the intellect is involved in thinking about feelings, attitudes, and values that it can become so complicated. People may have great potential for affective growth and confluent thinking, but they may presently be rationalizing and overintellectualizing ways to block their own progress. Statements like the following that may be valid in some circumstances may also be examples of masking a sense of threat or of anxiety about change.

1. "Don't overcomplicate matters. We've always known about the need to meet the public and our colleagues cordially and sympathetically. We need not study techniques to do so. Good manners suffice."

2. "Don't oversimplify. You are speaking of a very complex subject. A surface treatment such as this one will do us no good and may cause some harm."
3. "I wouldn't be me if I followed the suggestions you offer. I would have to force myself and it would be obviously contrived and artificial."
4. "This subject has nothing to do with me. I'm an acquisitions person" or "I'm a law librarian, not an educator or psychologist. I'm not the problem in this building anyway. It's Jane/Jim, who operates the terminal, who needs help."

The "Either-Or/More-or-Less" Syndrome

Many concepts and skills are presented in this book. If the reader has not dismissed them out of hand, he is probably wondering how to organize them in a coherent fashion. One tempting possibility is to fall prey to the all too human tendency to view them in an "either-or/more-or-less" manner. This legacy of bipolarity has haunted human thought through the ages. Indeed it is a common, albeit limiting, assumption that human traits, characteristics, and behaviors range along a number of specifiable bipolar dimensions. The variety of concepts presented herein could easily be cast into a series of bipolar dimensions. For instance, such dimensions could include cognitive/affective, autonomous/homonomous, rational/metaphoric, content/process, conscious/unconscious, and so forth.

The wide use of bipolar dimensions, however, is not without criticism. Lewin (1931, 1964) attributed this wide use to an adherence to the Aristotelian metatheory. Such a position reflects the ancient belief that all events in the universe were either heavenly or earthly, good or bad, valuated on a bipolar continuum. Loevinger (1965) argued that bipolarity is the result of historical accidents. The tendency to view human characteristics and processes in conjunction with their opposites is a function of both a language system and a conceptual process evident in many scientific fields. That is, one tends to view the infant as developing from dependency and passivity to independency and activity as a totality, just as one observes both anabolism (i.e., the process of changing food into living tissue) and catabolism (i.e., the process of changing living tissue into waste products of a simpler chemical composition) in the metabolic processes of living organisms. Once this accident occurred, it was then easy to commit a further blunder: if human characteristics or processes occur with their opposites and if there is a limited range of manifestations of such oppositional characteristics or processes (not a farfetched conclusion given the view of the finiteness of matter and of energy), then more of one necessarily means less of the other.

The ordering of an individual's behavior to a particular class does not imply that it is immutable. Nor does it imply that it is fixed or limited in quantity or in frequency. In fact, such behavior could also belong to another class different or opposite in meaning. Moreover, it could be highly variable in frequency and in quantity. One is hard pressed, for example, to conclude that an individual who displays dominant behavior in a certain situation is a dominant individual in all possible situations. Likewise, it is difficult to conclude that his dominance is fixed with regard to frequency and to quantity and thus restricts or limits his submissiveness. It makes better theoretical, empirical, and practical sense to ask under what conditions or in what situations is dominance displayed and in what quantity or with what frequency in those conditions or situations. Similar questions can then be asked regarding submissiveness independent of dominance.

Two research studies on core human characteristics bear mentioning. Beller (1959) presented clear-cut evidence that behaviors that are classified as dependent are not a priori nonindependent. Gonen and Lansky (1968) found that in addition to placing typical masculine and feminine behaviors on a bipolar continuum, people often use two other dimensions. The first is a masculinity dimension with *less masculine* and *more masculine* as end points; femininity is irrelevant. The second is a femininity dimension with *less feminine* and *more feminine* as end points; masculinity is irrelevant. Both studies support the argument against an exclusively bipolar view of human behavior.

The authors, therefore, want to avoid the bipolar trap in their discussion of the models, concepts, and skills summarized in this book.

The Common Threads: Confluence, Competence, and Creativity

The models presented in this book share the following beliefs:

1. That people are not powerless victims of their environment nor of their past; that they can choose to change their lives; and that they are responsible for the ways they conduct themselves.
2. That people are capable of showing concern, sharing, and loving; that they are not singletons, independent and heedless of each other.
3. That an individual's sense of self-esteem is related to interpersonal

contacts and to group experiences—including contacts and experiences in the family.

4. That not only the content of an individual's communication with another counts but also the processes used to communicate, the techniques employed to reach each other, count; that these are complex dimensions to the messages sent and received and to the interactions experienced.

5. That people's learning and experience have cognitive and affective components that are intertwined and equally important in determining who they are and how well they live as individuals and as members of any group.

6. That to the degree that people learn to acknowledge and utilize their cognitive and affective sides they become more confluent, more competent, and more creatively fulfilled as human beings.

7. That new dimensions of awareness and experience are available and accessible to people willing to put forth the effort to find them and work at them.

8. That people all have a need for competency in their interactions with others and in their dealings with the world; that communications skills provide the means to accomplish this competency.

9. That important links exist between cognitive and affective, between work and play, between creativity and productivity, and between the rational and the metaphoric.

The models presented provide the following:

1. A set of skills that allow individuals to examine thoughts, feelings, fantasies, intuitions, attitudes, and values.

2. Conditions that allow individuals to experience and appreciate their complexity and potential.

3. Increased competence in dealing with the self and with other people.

4. New ways to view human issues, to reframe human concerns, and to create conditions that allow change.

5. New and different ways to bring individuals together with groups.

6. Ways to strike a balance for the person as an individual and as a member of a group; that is, ways to exercise the needs for autonomy and for homonomy.

7. Methods to maximize an individual's creative potential, as well as a group's potential for synergy.

Three concepts emerge as central variables for the models described above. These are *confluence, competence,* and *creativity.* All the models provide both knowledge and skills that, when applied regularly and in combination, allow people to become and behave more integratedly, more competently, and more creatively. Figure 8 illustrates a matrix that summarizes and highlights some of the aspects of and relationships among the models and their functional tie-in with the three central variables: confluence, competence, and creativity. The authors have with forethought (malicious or otherwise) not included minor or "fringe" models, since their contributions are minimal at best and suspect at worst.

	Confluence	Competence	Creativity
Jones	1. Use of feelings, fantasies, and thoughts	1. Learning is more complete	1. Maximizes divergent and convergent thinking
	2. Focuses on outsight as well as insight	2. Stresses learning as relevant and thus it provides more impact	2. Deals with unconscious and preconscious processes (both part-and-parcel of the creative act)
	3. Focuses on the process, as well as the content of learning	3. Increases breadth and depth of learning	
Samples	1. Combines the metaphoric with the rational	1. Learning is not "half-minded"	1. Stresses analogy
	2. Develops the play-work sequence	2. Provides vehicles for increased understanding and for mastery	2. Argues for stimulating and using right-brain functions (as best science can determine, the seat of creative powers)
	3. Uses right-handed and left-handed approaches		
	4. Nonlinear and linear		

Figure 8.   Confluence, Competence, and Creativity: A Matrix for Comparing Communication Models

	Confluence	Competence	Creativity
Values Clarification	1. Develops the valuing process	1. Allows free choice in selecting values	1. Presents a multitude of activities using a number of modalities
	2. Integrates attitudes and values with learning of content and skills	2. Helps people be value clear and thus freer to transact with the world	2. Encourages play as a learning strategy
Rogers	1. Growth focused	1. Believes in the internal forces to grow, to change, to affect one's own life	1. Allows creative expression
	2. The "father" of a number of listening skills	2. Practices and allows congruence	2. Believes that learning occurs freely and that others can only facilitate creative approaches
	3. Accepts feelings 4. Stresses integrity		
Gestalt	1. Heavily feelings- and fantasy-focused	1. Integration allows more flexibility and choice	1. Uses imagery and dramatic techniques
	2. Stresses integration	2. Argues that completeness leads to mastery	2. Stresses the creation of events, of feelings, and of awareness
	3. Holistic		
Transactional Analysis	1. Integration of the three ego states	1. Understanding and insight	1. Stresses the importance of the Child ego state
	2. Physical and word strokes equally important	2. New learning about old decisions allows choices and redecisions	2. Process of uncovering material for change is playful

Figure 8 (*Continued*)

	Confluence	*Competence*	*Creativity*
	3. Words and feelings are basic	3. Adult ego state	3. Survival decisions (scripts) are creatively played out
	4. Verbal and nonverbal messages play a large role	4. Rewriting scripts and changing existential positions allow strength	
Effectiveness Training	1. Encourages use of and acceptance of feelings	1. Heavily skill oriented	1. Stresses divergent thinking regarding problem solving
	2. Helps clarify the vagaries involved in strong feelings	2. Concept of problem-ownership	2. Acknowledges each individual's ability to creatively deal with others and problems
		3. Problem solving focus	
		4. Allows choices	
Reality Therapy	1. Overlays a rational decision-making scheme on feelings and behaviors	1. Focuses on the issue of responsibility	1. Encourages involvement in many ways
	2. Requires value judgments regarding behaviors, thoughts, and feelings	2. Allows choices	2. Stresses brainstorming of alternatives
	3. Values equally giving and receiving love, self-worth, planning, and decision making	3. Helps develop skills in planning, decision making, and problem solving	3. Holds that very few situations are optionless

Figure 8 (*Continued*)

	Confluence	Competence	Creativity
Group Dynamics	1. Distinguishes between task functions and socioemotional functions	1. Provides skills for understanding and conducting groups	1. Synergy-process exceeds the sum of its members' skills and contributions
	2. Takes into account feelings, attitudes, and values	2. Focuses on leadership skills	2. Inherent growth and creative focus are in operation
	3. Ties formal aspects (roles and thinking) together with informal aspects (friendship patterns and feeling)	3. Gives a framework for viewing all human groups	3. Harnesses opposing forces to synthesize and to expand; to move on to different levels of experience
		4. Maximizes resources for dealing with all issues	
		5. Shared responsibility	

Figure 8 (*Continued*)

	Confluence	Competence	Creativity
Jones			
Samples			
Values Clarification			
Rogers			
Gestalt			
Transactional Analysis			
Effectiveness Training			
Reality Therapy			
Group Dynamics			

Figure 9. Extending the Matrix

Figure 8 represents only part of the complete picture. The reader is invited to try summarizing other aspects and relationships. The components of another matrix are provided in figure 9, including the central variables and the models. Take a few minutes and list other aspects and relationships. Remember that *confluence* is defined as integrating thoughts, feelings, fantasies, attitudes, and values into a meaningful whole. *Competence* is defined as having the ability to affect people, objects, and the environment, and *creativity* is defined as the ability to break sets, think divergently, see associations whether close or remote, and resynthesize by thinking convergently.

Future Directions

For the present, what the authors wanted to say about communication and peoplework has been said. They are aware, though, that the reader may just be beginning this long, involved, and at times confusing journey. With this mind, they want to leave the reader with some suggestions.

Effective human communication is difficult. It requires an attitude and a willingness to experiment. Not all the ideas given here will make sense in or will fit with an individual's situation or circumstances. The authors ask that the reader pick and choose, try out some of what has been shared. Each librarian knows best what needs to be done in an individual library or media center. Effective communication requires flexibility. Be eclectic! No one model or skill has all the answers. Avoid, at all costs, becoming trapped in the "true believer" syndrome. It is a well-researched and well-known fact that what an individual believes and/or expects will color greatly what he sees, does, and how successful he will be. Practice is important. Do not despair that any attempts are not perfect the very first time nor, for that matter, the fiftieth time. Have the courage to be imperfect—it is, after all, a very human thing to be. Most of all, do not panic. Effective communication takes time.

The authors recommend that the reader keep a journal of experiences. This might include descriptions of human events; thoughts, feelings, fantasies about affective communication; questions; and notes from any additional reading. Keep an ongoing plan for change; develop a worksheet. Possible categories for a worksheet are:

   I. The Situation.
  II. What I usually do.
 III. Does it work? What usually happens?
 IV. What I could do differently.
  V. Time Frame: How long do I give myself for each step?

Dealing with and effecting change is easier if an individual works with others. "Strength" does come with "numbers." Organize a support group. Remember, too, that a group is much, much more than the sum of its individual members. The natural synergistic forces of any group allow people to grow, learn, and change not only themselves, but also the people and the organizations around them. Trust these forces. Allow them to carry you and other members of your support group along the gentle streams of change.

As you survey your own library or media center, be aware of those around you. At the Purdue University library students and faculty who were touched while checking out materials reported more favorable views of the library and of the librarians than did those who were not touched (Fisher, Rytting, and Heslin, 1976; Heslin, 1976). Be aware of your language. Drop words from your vocabulary that deindividuate and dehumanize people who use your services (e.g., patron, user, etc.).

When you confront a problem, experiment. Reframe it. Consult an expert. Along those same lines, the authors have an offer. If you have a problem that cannot be resolved by your use of the models and skills in this book, write to them. They will do their best to provide assistance. And if all else fails, withdraw. It certainly is an option.

Make connections with colleges, universities, and community mental health centers in your area and with national groups listed below. There are people and programs available in humanistic psychology, communication skills and many other areas. Enroll in courses and workshops. Experience the workshops, experience the concepts, the skills, and the people first hand.

To those readers responsible and accountable for preparing and certifying librarians and administering libraries, develop courses and programs in conjunction with psychology departments, education departments, extension services, and/or continuing education divisions. Many people are willing to work with you.

For those interested in research, humanistic education for librarians is rich in possibilities. To date it has been neglected. Librarians should not continue to leave it unattended. There are many masters theses, doctoral dissertations, and publications waiting.

And finally, to all readers, the authors invite comments, criticisms, problems, and solutions that they have not anticipated or addressed. Good luck.

Some Resources

Association for Humanistic Psychology
325 Ninth Street
San Francisco, California 94103

National Humanistic Education Center
110 Spring Street
Saratoga Springs, New York 12866

National Training Laboratories
P.O. Box 9155
Rosslyn Station, Virginia 22209

University Associates
8517 Production Avenue
San Diego, California 92121

AN EXERCISE

Final and Eclectic

1. The new president of the board that governs youı library has decided that you, as library director, should speak out at a legislative hearing on pornography. She expects that you will speak in favor of a bill to ban pornographic literature. You feel this is diametrically opposed to the principles of library service. How will you go about making your position known to her? What would be the least threatening approach you could use in informing her of your position? How might you best deal with your own feelings about disclosure and confrontation?
2. There is a young boy who frequents the library who obviously does not have sufficient clothing for the winter. He has taken to surreptitiously stuffing newspapers into his shirt and the soles of his shoes. What can you do to help him?
3. In serving on a task force to design the curriculum for the state university's new graduate library school program, you realize that the offerings expected by the majority of the committee are those traditional courses that would be approved by ALA for accreditation. You feel that other, more innovative subjects must also be included in order to keep pace with the changes in the information sciences, the social sciences, and with the psychological needs of people who use libraries. How will you present your case? What forces will be at work to prevent your message from being accepted? What forces will help you to achieve your goal?
4. You are an active member of the regional library association that includes several states. Although the majority of members have not seen the film, this group feels that censure of ALA's *The Speaker* is in order. What steps would you take to determine your own position? What steps might you take to help the group reach a final decision?

5. As an administrator or department head of a large library system you unexpectedly find yourself the recipient of a vote of "no confidence" from your staff. This vote is based upon what the staff alleges is your lack of criteria for evaluation of their performance on the job. What ways could you use to discover how and why the staff perceives you with so little confidence? How will you deal with your feelings? How will you deal with the feelings of your staff?

6. Working late in the library one evening you discover an elderly woman huddled in a corner at the back of one of the stacks. She tells you that she has left a local nursing home and has no intention of returning there. How might you help her?

7. The young adults who use your library resent being relegated to a special room that houses only those books considered appropriate for adolescents. They wish to sit in other parts of the library and also read books from the general collection. The present policy was formulated by the board of trustees. Now a delegation of students wishes to challenge that policy. They have asked that you help them prepare a presentation and accompany them to the meeting. How do you feel about being placed in that situation? Will helping them hurt you in the eyes of the administration and the board? What kinds of help could you give them that would be least threatening to the board? How much responsibility do you feel you have in this situation? How much risk are you willing to take? Can you share your feelings with the students? With the board?

8. A small religious sect decides that the library is an "appropriate" place for their religious meetings. They have no church and the public library has a number of small meeting rooms. When you explain to them that the rules of the library restrict the use of meeting rooms, they assert that you are abridging their right to freedom of worship. They ask you to pray with them to help you to reconsider your position. What can you say to them that might help them accept the library regulation? What kind of behavior is best suited for this kind of confrontation? Would it be possible to use an I-message here?

9. A committee of local school teachers, school librarians, and public librarians have as their task planning the necessary changes to convert a large school library into a regional media center. Each of the people on the committee has different ideas about what a media center ought to be, what it ought to do, and whom it ought to serve. Each also represents widely divergent phi-

losophies of education and library science. As chairperson of this group, what will you do to help these people become a cohesive working group?

10. Circulation statistics and other factors indicate that the use of the neighborhood library is falling off. Within the past three years the area in which the library is located has rapidly deteriorated. The people who live in the neighborhood seldom use the library, while those who came in the past have started to use another branch. You have been charged by the head librarian with the responsibility of investigating the matter and recommending a course of action. What kinds of information do you need to have for your investigation? What steps would you take to complete this task?

References

Beller, E. K. Exploratory studies of dependency. *Transactions of the New York Academy of Science*, 1959, *21*, 414–26.

Fisher, Jeffrey D., Rytting, Marvin, and Heslin, Richard. Hands touching hands: Affective and evaluative effects of an interpersonal touch. *Sociometry*, 1976, *39*, 416–21.

Gonen, Jay Y., and Lansky, Leonard M. Masculinity, femininity, and masculinity-femininity: A phenomenological study of the *Mf* scale of the MMPI. *Psychological Reports*, 1968, *23*, 183–94.

Heslin, Richard. How people react to your touch. *Science Digest*. 1976, *79*, 46–56.

Lewin, Kurt. The conflict between Aristotelian and Galilean modes of thought in contemporary psychology. *Journal of General Psychology*, 1931, *5*, 141–77.

———. A dynamic theory of personality. In H. M. Ruitenbeck (ed.), *Varieties of personality theory*, pp. 196–234. New York: Dutton, 1964.

Loevinger, Jane. Measurement in clinical research. In B. B. Wolman (ed.), *Handbook of clinical psychology*, pp. 78–94. New York: McGraw-Hill, 1965.

Index

*Prepared by
Barbara Jacobs*

Design by Richard Pace
Composed by The Printing Department, University of Chicago
in Linotype Times Roman with Futura Light
and Helvetica display faces
Printed on 50# Warren's Olde Style, a pH neutral stock,
and bound by The Printing Department, University of Chicago